Praise for Jake Ducey a

"Once upon a time there were visionaries who formed Apple Inc., transforming the world—Steve Jobs and me. Now, Jake is here to transform the world in his own right."

—**Steve Wozniak,** cofounder of Apple Inc.

"Jake's journey and book are proof that when we follow the Law-of-Attraction, miracles become regularities and we live our wildest dreams while love surrounds us!"

—**Richard Cohn,** publisher of The Secret,
founder of Beyond Words Publishing

"This book will move you to pursue your wildest dreams."

—**Laird Hamilton,** World Surfing Champion

"This book shows that when we step Into the Wind, we naturally live life to glorify God."

—**Kenny Stills,** Nation's Top College Wide Receiver
for Oklahoma University.

"Jake's book shows that no matter your age, you can Think and Grow Rich, but that wealth begins within."

—**Greg S. Reid,** bestselling author, Napoleon Hill Foundation

"Jake's book shows that if you Make-A-Wish and act on it, you're rewarded. Inspiring!"

—**Frank Shankwitz,** founder of Make-A-Wish Foundation

"Jake's book, big vision, and unlimited passion will push you to do more to become a leader for a new way of life with endless possibilities."

—**Forbes Riley**, entrepreneur

"Jake's book is proof that when we trust in Spirit we achieve whatever we put our minds to, including changing the world."

—**Leah Amico,** three-time Olympic Gold Medalist,
motivational speaker

"Jake's youthful journey of speculation and inner transformation is a catalyst for his generation. His story is relatable to anyone, even your "average" teen or college student seeking a more fulfilling life. He is courageous in pursuing his spiritual evolution while activating others politically and publicly. Jake is a wonderful example of light and enlightened leadership."

—**Chanelle Sladics**, professional snowboarder, environmental activist, co-founder of simply straws, yogi

"With a raw, authentic passion for his mission, Jake Ducey is bringing New Thought principles of truth and love to a whole new generation of seekers. I'm so excited to watch the unfolding of this blossoming visionary."

—**Lisa McCourt,** author of *Juicy Joy: 7 Simple Steps to Your Glorious, Gutsy Self* and bestselling children's author

"Jake is a fearless and daring young man with a message and journey that'll make you leap off the edge of comfort to your destiny."

—**Nik Halik,** Thrillionaire, author and motivational speaker

"Jake's book and ability to speak will take you from your transition phase to one of success and purpose."

—**Johnny Campbell,** The Transition Man, Speaker Hall of Fame 2007

"Jake's adventures of illuminating past mistakes into divine greatness is an inspiration for anyone wanting to go beyond their negative mental conditioning."

—**Dr. David Corbin,** author, inventor, life coach

"Want inspiration to live the impossible dream? Read Jake's book. Listen to him speak."

—**David E. Stanley**, bestselling author, renowned public speaker

Into the Wind

Jake Ducey

Waterfront Publishing

By Jake Ducey
jakeducey.com
facebook.com/jakeduceyauthor

Published by Waterfront Publishing
Cardiff, California

ISBN: 978-1-939116-04-8

Printed and bound in the United States of America.

What on earth am I here for?

Contents

Foreword

Laird Hamilton

For me, life is about doing what has not been done. I believe that if people, especially young people, knew this was possible, they'd achieve the impossible.

Through my life I've come to experience that excuses and impossibilities drift away when we develop a certain attitude about life. By not accepting the world as is, but rather we mold it to our heart's desire. *Yes*, this can be a scary process, but I believe that fear can either paralyze us, or make us stronger.

It's clear to me that the latter can be anyone's reality if we step toward our fears that stand between us and our dreams. That is what I wish to share with the world—that we can't expect to ride the wave if we aren't even willing to catch it.

I saw this book *Into the Wind* after I met Jake, and believe it has an opportunity to truly deliver this message to many people, especially the younger generation.

Thus, it's exciting to see how different his book and journey are. Countless inspirational tales have been written, but few from a nineteen-year-old who left behind such a promising life, and even fewer who wandered the world without a map. This experience and wisdom he shares is relatable to all ages and inspires you to be the greatest you can be.

Jake proves that there is a better way to live by taking chances, humbling ourselves through experiencing fear, and riding what cannot be rode. This book will move you to pursue your wildest dreams.

—Laird Hamilton

Author's Note

This book was written for the sole intention of sharing what I discovered while wandering the world for six months: that we are more powerful than we've been led to believe and when we leap toward our destiny for the highest good of all, the whole world unfolds for us. Once we all do this, we *will* transform our world.

My journey is physical proof that each of us can set a goal and obtain it, that we *can* consciously create our realities, and that whatever we envision we *can* accomplish. This read will begin your path to realizing your personal dreams—that is, if you choose to pursue them.

Disclaimer: I have no disclaimer. By reading this book you will become aware that you are the creator of your own life, intentionally or unintentionally. You will know that we are going to change the world with this truth, eliminating all current threats to our future. Your world—our world—is about to change for the better. What you do with your individual responsibility is entirely your freewill of choice.

The world is a dangerous place to live;
not because of the people who are evil,
but because of the people who don't do anything about it.
—Albert Einstein

“Gambling with Dreams”

Well, she packed her bags, done left the country.
“There’s too much structure,” she’d say to me.
On that day she jumped into the wind.
Took a chance; she found herself as a friend.
Found stability in the unstable.
Learned to sense the universal life flow.
Before she left, this is what she said:
“There’s balance in the unknown,
To those who gamble with dreams,
Life is to be shown.”
Make a change, take a plane, or look within.
She told me not taking chances is sin.
Her heart didn’t want no more mundane tasks.
When her time comes due she wants the last laugh.
Don’t need to worry or fear, just be free.
That day I quit school and smashed my T.V.
Stopped caring what others think of me.
It’s the only way to live our destiny.
She questioned, “What do you really need?”
But I hadn’t given thought to my dreams.
And that’s the most common failure we see.
Before she left, this is what she said:
“There’s balance in the unknown,
To those who gamble with dreams,
Life is to be shown.”

—Jake Ducey

Acknowledgments

I would like to acknowledge and dedicate this book to my grandfather, Clark. He has instilled in me since childhood the belief that whatever we can think, believe, and act upon, we can deliberately create as reality. Here is to you, Papa. I've realized my dreams.

Also, this is to my mother, father, and brother.

Also, to the nearly 7 billion people across this world—many unnamed humans have aided me. If you have, then this book is my offering back to you for your generosity. If not, then consider this the first offering toward friendship between us.

I am also grateful to the Western world for the freedoms that have granted me the opportunity to write this.

And I am in debt to the wind for blowing me as far as I have come.

A book is not an individual achievement but a collaborative effort. I would like to especially thank the following people; Laird Hamilton (for showing me what a role model is), Chanelle Sladics (for too many things to name), Duncan Barnes (graphic designer), Faith Dendt (designer), Carol Rosenberg (editor), Kjersti Buass (who picked out all my business clothes), Micky Wiswedel and Donez (My Photographers), Barry Mack (original designer), Jill Mangino (Publicist), Bill Gladstone (Agent), Vanessa Chalmers, The Rawbrahs (Mentors/Inspirations), Sean Stephenson (Mentor), Greg S. Reid (Mentor), and Marianne Williamson (one of my heroes).

When you are inspired by some great purpose, some extraordinary project, all your thoughts break their bonds, your mind transcends limitations...and you find yourself in a new and wonderful world, dormant forces, facilities and talents come alive and you discover yourself to be a greater person than you ever dreamed.

—Patanjali

Part One

USA: Choose

Enough Is Enough

Los Angeles, California, November 20, 2010

> *Remembering that I'll be dead soon is the most important tool I've ever encountered to help me make the big choices in life.*
>
> —Steve Jobs

The journey of thousands of miles began with a choice. I had to decide what I wanted from life: to die with a dream inside of me or to live it while I could. I chose the latter. The rest became what some call destiny.

I was lost, aimlessly pacing along an old dusty road for years. One paved with prescription pills, a college basketball scholarship, and no genuine happiness. I hadn't known where it was taking me until I came upon it. Now this road is no longer dusty. It appears my journey has just begun. It's as if I now know where I am going. And I know I am getting closer.

It is said that no reward comes without risk, and so I took one. I can still see the day I rolled life's dice and gambled on my dreams. I had known what I wanted. Because of this the world brought it to me. And it happened with so much speed it all doesn't seem real anymore. *I* created my reality.

Within my memory is the birth of my adventures. This took place in Economics 101 at California Lutheran University on November 20, 2010.

"Am I boring you, Mr. Ducey?" Dr. Mills interrogated me with a microexpression of frustration.

"No, sir, I apologize for yawning," I countered with a smile so apologetic a human wouldn't dare to look and not forgive. "It's not that I am uninterested…" I paused and looked around at the whiteboard covered in numbers. "It's that I'm so captivated and enthralled I forgot to breathe!"

I explained how I had recently read an article in *Scientific Magazine* that talked about how yawns aren't merely symbols of fatigue but also signs of unrestrained enthusiasm. As the situation unfolded, I discovered that my teacher had also read the story. He nodded in acknowledgment of the truth.

Nevertheless, I may have been exaggerating reality just then. I was not consumed in dialogue I found important. My concentration was dwindling. My teacher had no answer to the question I had asked moments before. I had wondered why the American people couldn't legally audit the Federal Reserve, who controls our money flow, especially during a recession. I thought it was a simple question. It was about economics, in a *real* economics class. Even so, he had no answer and swiftly swapped subjects to the necessity of the bank bailouts we were still in the midst of during the fall of 2010.

"Please, Jake, fancy your curiosity during your free time, but now questions must be pertinent to what we are learning in the book!"

I painstakingly nodded, looking at the white walls. I thought back to high school when I had been an outstanding student. My junior-year English teacher would often send me to *stand out* of the classroom as punishment for being so outstandingly troublesome. Now while I was stuck sitting in this classroom, I debated whether or not to fake a seizure.

I watched my professor earnestly, wondering if he knew of my secret plan. My body coursed with frustration, and his halfhearted smile gave me little reassurance. In a financial class, I thought the answer to why we can't audit the people who print our money was as vital as asking a spiritual master about the meaning of life. Paradoxically, that didn't seem to be the case. As a result, I closed my eyes. I was pretending I wasn't there anymore. It was then that I yawned.

I sat chained to a little wooden chair within a little white classroom, writing with a little yellow pencil on a little white piece of paper with only a little bit of sanity left to hold back my shrieks. I didn't want to learn how to be another number. I wanted to know how we were going to fix the financial catastrophe destined to affect my generation. Moreover, I thought the point of life was to do what we love, not what we are forced to do.

It was then that I knew I didn't want to be the man in a suit and tie pounding three cups of coffee per day just to stay afloat in a job that was anything less than my dreams.

I was nineteen years old. The sensitive spot of my attention was asking to be tickled. I knew nothing justified the sacrifice of not loving what one did during the most mentally and physically capable years of life, regardless of age.

While I spun the pencil between my thumb and index finger, I found no reason to blame my teacher for shrugging off my question. I actually felt compassion for him. Perhaps he didn't know because no one did. Similar to how no one knows what the invisible source that creates subatomic particles is made of. Just as we don't know where thoughts come from or how powerful we all *really* are.

It wasn't by coincidence that all of the aforementioned were questions in my mind. By then, I was too absorbed in waves of inspiration telling me to travel a different life road, with a different mind. Each hair on my arm stood as firm as a motivational speaker, telling me I was entitled to experience my full potential, that all of us are.

"The principle that governs all life says that the world will manifest whatever one aspires to as long as they make the choice about what they want and then act upon it for the highest good of all," said a voice in my head.

I slid off my sandals and tasted an unpalatable lungful of the overcrowded classroom air. I focused on my out breath. Deep down my inner being knew there was so much more to experience than what I'd been told by our Western society. I was submersed in an environment where everyone followed the house rules. But I didn't want to play the game anymore. I wanted to be myself. Still, I wasn't quite sure who I was.

My reflection offered no insight. I was aware that peering into a mirror could be a terrifying experience when one isn't ready for the truth within. But I wanted to know it and had been self-directing my own learning for almost two years. I desired to see beyond the limitations of the mirror and perceive what exists beyond shapes, contours, lines…well into the hereafter.

Just then, navy-blue words spilled like ink onto my page of notes:

Why are you not following your dreams?
How can you break the bars on this purposeless prison?
How do you expect the world to change
if you don't follow your heart?

I contemplated the message. Where I lived, people walked on paved streets with their feet. I didn't have a desire to walk on my hands; I just wanted to wander in places without paved streets and molded minds. A change in latitude might take me there.

That day when economics class was over, I stepped outside. I walked slowly down the concrete steps, grasping the yellow guardrail. I looked up into the clouds, knowing that my friend Tyler was waiting for me in the grass ahead. As I walked toward him, my mind journeyed backward three years to October 25, 2007.

> *I could see myself trying to push the SUV back onto its wheels, as if I could really do it. No use. It was upside down. It only stopped rolling when it hit the cement sewage tank.*

In my state, I thought the 1995 Toyota 4-Runner was still in mint condition. Perhaps my parents wouldn't notice that most of the roof was missing.

Or that the windows were all broken.

Or that my hands were bleeding.

Moments earlier, I'd punched out the windshield and crawled out of the vehicle.

"Hey, kid, are you alright?" a man shouted as he approached the accident. "You flipped your car four times!"

"Wasn't me. It was the car. And the car is fine," I joked.

He looked at me sideways. He didn't believe me.

I noticed the beer cans at my feet. A couple dozen had tumbled from the car during the accident. I stumbled to pick a few up and threw them into the bushes. Why, I don't know. By and by, I assumed that all the Xanax I'd been carrying had also been lost in the accident, and I hoped for a similar fate with my fake ID.

I was some forty feet below Encinitas Boulevard, a half mile from my high school. I had been drinking since midday. At 7:55 pm my front left wheel had clipped the center median. The SUV rolled four times across the three eastbound lanes, tore through the steel roadside barrier, and flipped down the ravine.

I looked around for my passenger. My friend, Jonny, was in the bushes, feet in the air. He had been tackled by a man who thought he was fleeing the scene. He wasn't dead, and neither was I. Or at least I didn't feel dead.

I closed my eyes, rubbed my head, unknowingly washing my blond hair with my blood.

> *The next time I opened my eyes, I was in a hospital bed in the emergency room. I was too drunk and worried to listen to everything the cop was saying, but I did hear that I had a blood alcohol level of 0.16. I remember thinking it was the same number as my age. I also remember thinking that I was lucky to be alive.... It scared me to death to know how close I had come to dying. So frightened was I that I wanted to forget that any moment of any day can be the last moment we spend here on earth.*

I shook the dream from my head, and Tyler came into view. I'd revisit it again in another flashback, some other time, as I always did. For now, all I needed to remember was that what had once frightened me into forgetfulness now liberated me: *We can be dead in a moment's notice, so we must follow our hearts.*

"Yo, Jake!" Tyler said from the ground. "You okay? You were spacing out!"

When I reached him, I gave him a slight smile. "I can't do this anymore, man!" I said. "I'm going to travel the world. I don't know where I'm going. I'm just going to do something different. I'm going to find out why I'm here on this earth."

Tyler stood up and patted me on the shoulder. I knew he didn't believe me. I didn't care. I knew that if I wanted to follow my dreams, I'd have to be independent of other people's opinions.

That evening was one of those no-moon nights when the cosmic crescent is devoured prematurely by the hungry sky. While I watched darkness feast on the glowing gem, I saw no reason to wait until I was sixty and retired with arthritis and thirty years of a nine-to-five job in order to experience life and understand myself. It became clear to me that we have inalienable rights as residents of this earth to step beyond our fears of trying new things. Thus, I knew I had to take control of my life, because it's our responsibility to find out what happiness *really* means to us, all the while admitting and surrendering to the fact that everything isn't as serious as it's made out to be.

Later, sleep swept through the blankets on my bed while I questioned myself: *To try or not to try? To find myself or blend in? If not now, then when?*

Before my body drifted into sleep I swore by the force of life within me that I *would* follow my own path and see where it led. I did not know that I was destined to scale the summit of my being.

The principle that governs all life says that the world will manifest whatever we aspire to as long as we make the choice about what we want and then act upon it for the highest good of all.

Making an Intention

Los Angeles, California, November 22, 2010

> *Your task is not to seek for love, but merely to seek and find all the barriers within yourself that you have built against it.*
>
> —Rumi

Some nights after that day in economics class, I stood in my bedroom peering into the full-length mirror for a glimpse of the truth. As much as I wanted to, I couldn't see beyond my curly-headed six-foot-three-inch frame. I tried smiling at myself, but I knew the gesture was mostly insincere. Soon, I completely lost sight of myself behind the rising smoke from the codeine-laced joint between my fingers. I stepped through the cloud closer to the mirror and stared into my blue eyes. They were red. The left one was shutting by itself. I rubbed it a few times, but that only made it worse.

My present situation symbolized my state of being. I couldn't see all of who I was behind the obscure smoke of aimless living. There I stood, continuing to numb myself from my life—one in which I lacked purpose. Waking up each day to study subjects I disliked and found no value in was dampening my passion for life. I had again started to mask my lack of joy with life-sucking drugs like codeine, Valium, and cocaine—somehow using that to avoid the truth I had learned in the car crash: *We'll be dead soon and need courage to live our dreams now.*

It frightened me, but somewhere deep within, untouched by the woes of the outside world, a part of me knew that we are born to be happy and successful. We're here for a mission. Our existence is no fluke of nature, no accident. My heart knew for certain that life had a unique purpose in mind for each of us when we were created and that our purpose extends *far beyond* anything we can imagine. This purpose is the True Love for life: being a willing instrument for a task recognized by each one of us as a significant one for the highest good of all.

I sat down on the blue carpet. Some binders were scattered by my feet. I debated throwing them away. Although I knew the answers to the questions my teachers asked, they weren't the answers I was looking for. As the thought dawned on me that I was wasting my life, salty tears dripped down my cheeks. I put my face down on the carpet and prayed for help.

I took a deep breath and regained composure. My soul knew the importance of being a positive force of nature rather than an agitated, nervous, and selfish person without inspiration who feels depressed and complains that life won't make him happy. Yet that was what I was doing, despite all of the life-affirming messages I had accumulated from my favorite authors. I was afraid to put into practice what I'd learned from teachers such as Wayne Dyer, Tony Robbins, Marianne Williamson, Eckhart Tolle, Gabrielle Bernstein, Victor Villasenor, Jack Canfield, and Deepak Chopra. Instead, I was sitting in classrooms "memorizing textbooks." It felt like the world was shaping me instead of me shaping myself.

Still, I knew that we each have the ultimate say in how our life will go and how happy we can be. I was also realizing there's a difference between *learning it* and *living it*. *Learning it* means waking up every day knowing you're doing something less than your wildest dreams. *Living it* means courageously stepping toward your wildest dreams, even if you don't know where to begin.

Making the complacent choice of *learning it* took me to rock bottom in my first semester of college. That's when I turned to self-help books for a better understanding of life. Over the course of two years, these books helped me recognize that our cultural norm is to give up our power to things outside ourselves. Most of us give our attention to Hollywood, math tests, paychecks, movies, television, and the government. When this happens we naturally begin to think that greatness is something only special people have or that we must somehow acquire it from outside ourselves. Yet it is already within us.

I was still looking outside myself for happiness (it felt easier to do what everyone else was doing), even though I had learned that all of the most influential people in history did not conform to the ideals of society: Albert Einstein, John Lennon, Ralph Waldo Emerson, Gandhi, Socrates, and Martin Luther King Jr. And so I continued to chase, and I fell, and I chased, and I fell—for the love of women, for the love of drug-induced pleasure, and for the love of social status and accolades from money and college degrees. Always I was brought back to depression, anger, lack of motivation, and resentment. It made me feel as if I never did anything right and that I wasn't good enough.

Since the primary cause of unhappiness is never the situation but our thoughts about it, then it's no wonder I felt uneasy. For one reason or another, I wasn't always able to connect the dots. As a result, I often blamed everything except myself for my own discontent, never realizing that by pointing blame, I gave up my power.

I rolled onto my back. My body was sore and tired. I looked up at the smooth white ceiling. A voice told me that the knots in my body were from "not's" in my belief system. I closed my eyes and reflected on my struggles over the past year and a half of college—blacking out at parties, losing my wallet, waking up in absolute fear.... This type of behavior obviously wasn't bringing me happiness. I'd just been too scared to fully admit that my own heart was the purest conduit for all I wanted. I knew that by acknowledging such a truth, my whole life would radically change. I feared such change.

If we are open to it, a time comes in each of our lives when we stop waiting for the person we want to become and start being the one we want to be. Something inside me knew that. I had clearly hit all the brick walls in the how-to-find-happiness book. I decided it was time to quit learning and start doing. I stood up and tossed the joint into the toilet. That would be the last time I'd use drugs to cover up a deeper emotional situation. I didn't know why it never occurred to me that such hard drugs could never bring me love. It was then I decided that when we love ourselves we'll always be loved. I was also done reading self-empowerment books about how powerful my mind was. I could no longer ingest any more beliefs about what I was capable of. I had to *experience* it.

I sat back on the carpet, closed my eyes, and began focusing on my breath. I smiled, recognizing that the only way to break free is to realize that we already are all that we seek. We aren't separate from anything, not even our dreams. I only had to accept and love who I already was and not try to be someone else. Then the whole world would unfold for me.

Opening my eyes, I reached for my notebook and pen. I would write down my thoughts, these new affirmations, to reprogram my mind. I flipped to a blank page and wrote: "I can do anything. I am provided for by life, I am..."

When the last words hit the paper, something clicked in my heart. It was as if a higher part of my brain suddenly became active.

"This is nothing I don't already know!" I exclaimed aloud, even though I was the only one in the room with whom I could share my epiphany.

I realized then that I had only needed to prove it to myself. I had just forgotten it when I was raised in this world where we aren't taught that we *really* are geniuses. But now I remembered.

Time strode on. My belief that I knew best for myself became stronger. As a result, I respectfully questioned *everything* I had been told. Thus, I lost friends because I became a nemesis to the comfort they pursued. And professors, like my economics one, quit trying to answer the difficult questions that were on my mind. I could see clearly that my campus was no longer a place that served my highest good. I was becoming aware that truth doesn't come from hierarchies, as we think, but from our own hearts.

Since opportunity wasn't knocking in college life, I realized I would have to build my own door. Fortunately, I began to see that I was here on this earth to go beyond my old limitations. I knew I'd never pick through the previous night's garbage to cook the following day's meal. Therefore, I saw no reason to live from old self-destructive behaviors. It was time to admit that coins and minds (especially confused ones) can always flip, but that hearts can never turn if we listen to them.

The sun rose the same way as it had on previous days, yet life began speaking to me in a different fashion: "When nothing goes right, go left," it seemed to say.

Being that we are *all* different, life guided *me* the following week to buy a plane ticket to Guatemala. It wasn't that school was wrong; it just wasn't right for me at this time. Leaving behind all that I knew to discover what I did not know was something I knew I *had* to do. I was trusting my intuition, though it rendered me no reason. And for months I had been studying the Mayan culture and their shamans in a sacred mountain town called Lake Atitlan. I felt compelled to be there. I wanted to experience the world from a completely different point of view.

I knew very little Spanish, and so my brother, Cole, and my roommate, Colton, who spoke fluent Spanish, offered to accompany me as translators for the first two weeks. Both twenty-four-year-old entrepreneurs, they were also seeking inspiration and clarity on their missions to construct their own start-up companies. Afterward, they would return home to San Diego, while I journeyed the world solo.

I had a hypothesis to prove: We all can live our destiny by following our hearts.

I hadn't a clue how long I would ultimately wander for, but I figured the $8,000 I'd saved since childhood would last me a good while if I spent it carefully. I'd begin in Guatemala, and then head toward Australia. I was feeling drawn there and suspected that it would give me balance before I headed to Asia.

Previously, I had planned to use my savings for necessities such as off-campus rent, gas, and food. Yet I no longer wished to plan for *that* future. I was aware that our world is *now* in a crisis and in need of new ideas to evoke global transformation and peace. Thus, I wanted to risk everything and see where the wind of chance would blow me.

It was then for the first time that I officially asked life to provide for me. By and by, it was the first time I ever gave full trust to the world to take care of me. And having spent the majority of my existence attempting to experience the future or relive the past, I was soon to know that in between those two extremes is life itself. Thus, wandering in the moment became a way for me to reestablish the original accord that had once existed between life and me.

There's a difference between *learning it* and *living it*. *Learning it* means waking up every day knowing you're doing something less than your wildest dreams. *Living it* means courageously stepping toward your wildest dreams, even if you don't know where to begin.

Part Two

Guatemala: Take Action & Believe

Fear Isn't Real

Guatemala City, December 21, 2010

"Come to the edge," he said.
They said, "We are afraid."
"Come to the edge," he said.
They came. He pushed them…and they flew.
—Guillaume Apollinaire

Sometime after midnight the wheels of the metal bird screeched to a stop on the landing strip. Even if my feet weren't yet touching Guatemala's land, this was my first time experiencing distant foreign soil. My heart beat quickly. I felt unusually alive, thankful for each breath. My hands were sweaty with excitement. I rubbed them on my brown corduroys before noticing my thoughts had changed, as if the shift in latitude gave me a more positive attitude. With Cole and Colton along, I wasn't too concerned that my Spanish was off—a mixture of unyielding eye contact, excessive brow movements, and hand motions I'd picked up from three years of sign language, with an occasional fluent splotch of Spanglish.

I arched my back and lifted my shoulders like a cobra from the blue cushion that airlines call a seat. The Guatemalan next to me, Enrique, was confused as we prepared to exit. He was a college student with skin that was chocolate-mocha from his years in the tropical sun. Paradoxically, at that moment in time, his face was pale and thunderstruck. He stumbled, fumbling through his bits and bobs of luggage, probably absorbed in thoughts surrounding the exchange of ideas he'd had with Colton before the plane began to descend.

Enrique had invited us to a party: "Twenty-four-hour rave the night of the full moon with everything you can imagine. Girls galore!" he told us.

I smiled, not so much at him, but to myself. The folly of it made me laugh inside. But Colton laughed aloud and told Enrique that our generation has a mission to change the world. That being said, we hadn't traversed continents to tip back bottles and belly flop into hotel pools, even if they were overflowing with women of mesmerizing majesty. No, not us. Not this time around.

Personally, I had a dream and I needed to manifest it. If I'd lost sight of my goal, I would've lost my way. Cole, Colton, and I had traveled to this place by agreement to ingest the heavenly concentration of volcanic mountains that imploded on themselves epochs ago, forming a Mayan lake home to twelve ancient villages called Lake Atitlan. We hoped for shamanic insight on how to utilize our own power.

So when we responded to Enrique's offerings of unrestrained indulgence with news of our plans, it was as if he were seeing snow fall in the middle of the relentless Guatemalan summer.

"Are you sure you are Americans?" he asked again as we all headed toward the international arrivals gate.

We nodded. In response, Enrique tripped on his shoelace and tumbled over his carry-on luggage. Relatively short but built like a tank, Colton graciously lifted our confused Guatemalan friend up and stationed him firmly on the polka-dotted carpet. We thanked him for his offer and wished him well before continuing onward.

Some thousands of moments later, I clicked my heels on the cement of the taxi-waiting zone. I turned to Cole, who was on his cell phone making a call to the homestay that was *supposed* to be our night's resting place. They weren't answering. It was after one in the morning. That meant only a handful of taxis were left and even fewer homestays were open.

The clean air drifted through my nose and alleviated any panic about having nowhere to stay. I knew that when we remove our fears of the unknown from seemingly vulnerable situations by courageously stepping toward them, balance can be found in the instability. Fear is created from the anxiety we have when faced with events outside our control. What we can *always* control, though, is the way we define these experiences. By simply shifting our focus, we can turn "problems" into opportunities for growth. Our choice has the power to determine the emotion we bring into any experience, whether it's excitement, love, or fear.

I reminded myself of all of this as I stood on the curb across from a row of two-story concrete buildings. A few cars drove past. The air was thick with moisture, yet comfortably warm. We rested inside the steel gate of the waiting zone. I laughed, feeling a bit like a zoo animal. The few dozen Guatemalans outside the airport watched us curiously. We were the only white-skinned people among them.

"Taxi?" a Guatemalan man with salt-and-pepper hair and a Bob Marley T-shirt asked us in half Spanish, half English. We looked at him curiously. Then we looked at each other. There was no other option. The tyrant tick of the clock was creeping toward morning.

We piled into the old beige sedan and were celebrated with the taxi driver's loud laughter. "You fly in tonight and don't have a place to stay? There are only three places to sleep in zone thirteen of Guatemala City this late."

We explained to him that we had made plans for accommodations, and Cole gave him the address of the homestay. The driver laughed again. As he pulled away from the curb, he introduced himself as Pablo and welcomed us to his country.

The stone street made for a bumpy ride; I bobbed up and down on the tattered seat. I licked my hand to wipe away the heap of dust from the back window so I could look out. I peered at the silhouettes of the armed guards who stood watch at the barbed-wire checkpoints. I hadn't witnessed a sight like this before.

I thought the vast differences between here and my hometown might cause me to spontaneously combust from culture shock. I imagined how it would sound on the six o'clock news back home: "Local teenager explodes into astronomical dust upon landing in Guatemala! Now, here's Tom with the weather…"

I twirled my fingers through my hair with a smile, vowing not to defy the laws of physics on the first night out of my country. *Maybe later,* I thought.

A few minutes later, the taxi came to a clanking halt beside the curb a few feet outside the homestay where we *had* reserved a room. A single light shone from above the concrete-fenced patio. I noticed the blue of the Guatemalan flag dangling in the windless night.

I opened the taxi door hurriedly and regretted it immediately because it sounded as if I'd pulled it off the hinges. I was relieved to see I didn't.

The wind was asleep. I looked around at the old white two-story concrete building. A huge steel gate about ten feet high fenced the property. It was on the corner of two vacant streets that intersected each other—coursed with apartments that were covered in high, slightly cracked, concrete walls and/or barbed-wire fences.

Pablo pressed the doorbell for what seemed like forever, while I played with the disturbing idea of sleeping on the cement. Then he spoke: "No aqui. Not here. Only two homestays left in town."

It sounded to me as if he had said, "No agua," and for a moment, I felt reassured. I could do without water for the night.

Colton and Cole quickly set me straight, and I grinned. I fell in line behind Pablo, who had motioned for us to follow him. He led us down a stone path behind the building toward another homestay. It was a small pathway that intersected the buildings and led to a different street. When we arrived at the next homestay, it looked just like the first except that here the bamboo door was adorned with a gold-and-black painting of the Mayan gods of creation. I couldn't help but smile at the synchronicity of such a sighting. There I was, seeking out the truth of life in a far-off land, and I had the Mayan gods of creation escorting me through the darkness.

The man who answered the door said that all beds were occupied. The door closed and locked. The wind randomly gusted—that was all. I laughed and was surprised by my own patience.

"We can sleep back in the airport," my brother told Pablo with the sunny smile that always cleared my clouds in childhood.

"No! No! Airport closed now for night! Cerado," Pablo replied.

We wandered a hundred yards down the vacant road. I wondered if the answers to life I sought waited somewhere down that path. We stopped at the last place that offered accommodation in the city at such a time of night. The place looked much more like an upper-class multiple-story residential home. It was painted white with brown windowpanes. There was a small white gate with black metal bars and a front patio with an old stone fountain. The water trickled lightly, easing my mind. And although this homestay looked more alive than the others, it still seemed to be asleep.

I walked nearer to the wall, spontaneously talking to it a bit, asking it to awaken the people inside, careful that this odd behavior would not be noticed by my companions.

No lights of salvation were shining through the windows. We took a few steps along the circular stone path, which ended at a locked gate. Our predicament still stood. The intercom on the side of the gate rang for minutes as Pablo continued to press it. A mental fire of worry should've been blazing, but the three of us just laughed. We were ready for complications that would test our patience, humility, and flexibility.

Crack! Crack!

The locks opened. A light of refuge flickered on. A gracious woman appeared in the distance by the front door. She walked down the few steps and through the patio. Unbolting the gate, she spoke with a humorous tone, "I am so sorry for the wait.... You boys nearly had to sleep on the concrete!"

I smiled, but I was not surprised. When we don't worry, everything works out. Life has no intention of punishing anyone for making the choice to follow their heart.

We said good-bye to our new friend Pablo, who seemed as relieved as we were that we had a place to sleep, and arranged for him to pick us up in the morning for the three-hour drive to Lake Atitlan.

When we remove our fears of the unknown from seemingly vulnerable situations by courageously stepping toward them, balance is found in the instability. Fear is created from the anxiety we have about events outside our control. What we can *always* control, though, is the way we define these experiences. With this attitude, we can turn "problems" into opportunities of growth by simply shifting our focus. Our choice has the power to determine the emotion we bring into any experience, whether it's excitement, love, or fear.

No Coincidences, Only Synchronicity

Lake Atitlan, December 22, 2010

> *Everything is Energy and that's all there is to it. Match (and sustain) the frequency of the Reality you want and you cannot help but get that Reality. It can be no other way. This is not Philosophy. This is Physics.*
>
> —Albert Einstein

At six in the morning Pablo's smile was so energizing it would have superseded the need for Guatemala's freshly ground organic coffee, if I wasn't already drinking it.

"For you, Pablo, from all of us," I said, offering him a brand-new Bob Marley T-shirt while we loaded up his taxi in the driveway. When I packed my bags before leaving the country I had filled it only with Bob Marley T-shirts and plain white ones; I wanted to send a message of peace and wisdom to whomever saw me.

Pablo held the shirt up in the early cool blue sky, the way Mufasa did with Simba in the *Lion King*. Then he gave each of us a nearly suffocating bear hug. It was better than any words he could've uttered. The cloudless sky was an omen of good things to come. We knew our new friend would steer us away from any typical trouble a tourist might encounter. We piled into his taxi once again. My brother sat in the front, while Colton and I were in the back. I popped my head out the window like a dog to be sure I didn't miss a single sight.

Watching children sit nearly naked in the dirt made me instantly realize that we Westerners are a peculiar breed. In many ways, from birth, we have been given the golden opportunity to fulfill our potential and change thousands of lives...if we choose to uncover who we are and why we're here. Meanwhile, these people seemed to have none of the basic civil liberties that all humans should be entitled to. There was a degradation of their heritage from an upsurge of Western jungles of glass, concrete, and steel high-rises all through Guatemala City. Texaco, Shell, and McDonald's sprouted out of nowhere on the streets. The buildings split the sky. As we wandered along in that taxicab, I wondered how it all came to be. I watched the clouds pass by. I was relieved to see that they hadn't cut them down as well.

When we made it to the countryside, I pressed my face against the window. Green mountains climbed the sky only to plummet into small streams. The sights energized me. Rivers coursed in circles like shining ribbons across the highlands like an optical illusion. I tracked one up the mountain until I saw a separate waterway, rushing some 180 degrees downward in another direction. Then I tried to peer inside the roadside homes that resembled the tree houses I'd played in as a kid in my backyard before dinner. I could almost hear my mother call my name for supper. I tried to imagine who I would've become if I'd never had the privileges I had in my world. I couldn't.

I continued to watch my surroundings while we winded up the tree-covered mountains, watching the little "villages" of Mayans—who lived on the dirt shoulders of the road. Their fruit stands were lean-tos made out of tin and a few pieces of wood. Their homes seemed to be the backside of the shops.

I leaned my head against the seat. When I closed my eyes, I could see my dreams unfolding. Recalling what Colton said on the flight to Guatemala, I smiled: "Most of us are busy gambling on the most dangerous risk of all—living our whole life not doing what we want on the bet that we can buy the freedom to do it later."

His statement had me determined to find my freedom now. *I am an explorer,* I supposed silently. *An explorer in search of how to turn my dreams into reality, and it's worth wasting tens of thousands of days over.*

"Jake? Jake? Anyone in there?" Cole asked, poking my stomach.

I opened my eyes. "I was out like a rock," I responded, not ready to share my thoughts out of fear they would vanish like a dream when one awakens to the morning sun. I looked out the window for the first time in forty minutes. I saw a lake that mirrored the sun's rays in a way that made it look like a bathing pool between heaven and earth. Some six thousand feet above sea level, three volcanoes covered in green bush rose above the water. At the base of them were many small towns with stout buildings.

"Panajachel, mi amigos. This is the main town of Lake Atitlan," Pablo said before we paid him fifteen dollars and hugged him good-bye.

Shoeless children lined the stone street near the dock. A group of them were kicking around a deflated soccer ball. The smiles on their faces made me wonder which of us was the rich one, them or me. It was then that I realized if we want to feel wealthy we need only to count all the things we have that money can't buy.

Small wooden *tiendas,* or stores, lined the central street. Ice cream signs hung on white wooden walls. It was the lowest priced food, besides chips. Six or seven wooden shops sat adjacent to one another, selling the exact same items. A few groups of five or ten men stood in circles talking about what I assumed was how they'd get us to buy stuff. It wasn't a dubious assumption to make, as moments later they were pulling on our arms, calling us family, and showing us bags of sunglasses and red Mayan blankets.

The main way of transportation between the twelve villages around the lake was by dinghy. We walked to the wooden dock that was hardly big enough to tie two boats to it. Our stop was destined to be across the water in the town of San Marcos, a place said to have powerful healing energies.

Colton, Cole, and I walked along the rustic and wobbly dock to a tiny wooden boat. Seven or eight men ushered us with urgency. The three of us climbed in and putted away slowly with the driver. The boat skimmed along. We all prayed it wouldn't sink while we laughed.

The Central American sun massaged my face and set ablaze any lingering troubles and worries. There were no cares, just a mind full of dreams that I knew would become reality.

The lush, vibrant landscape, which made for a peaceful illustration, pleased my inner being. Three green volcanoes watched over the blue lake while smoke from the restaurants sailed above the towns nestled below the lush peaks.

"From the sight of it all, one would think our creator had only three fingers," said our skipper, Emanuel, in English.

I looked at him curiously, as it was one of the most poetic things I'd ever heard. I nodded enthusiastically at his comparison of the three volcanoes tips to God's fingers. Then, the bobbing of my head corresponded with the flight path of a pair of hawks overhead.

"Guys, do you know what that means?" I asked excitedly, pointing at the hawks. "Two of them hovering in the sky like that symbolize messages to the natives. It must mean we are going to meet our shaman soon!" I drummed on the wooden seat for effect and let out a hearty laugh.

Emanuel responded, "Drums are the heartbeat of the earth." Then he banged on the bottom of the dinghy, chanting a Mayan mantra we didn't understand. Water sprayed us while we listened in silence for a few moments. When he was finished, he explained, "It means to be one with the Earth and all beings." He paused and looked at us with a wide grin. "We are here to break through our illusions of separation. Like the morning's rising sun, there is a new way of life creeping in slowly.... Those who embrace it will begin to thrive."

The boat drifted into a horde of palm trees along the shoreline of our intended destination. Amid friendly faces, we hopped off the boat onto the grassy shore. The tropical, humid air felt good on my skin. A handful of lounge chairs and colorful hammocks were nestled among blue and yellow flowers, small palm trees, and green bushes dotted with purple berries. I eyed what would become my favorite spot—a hammock just below a banana tree. It was only a stone's throw away from the lake.

Just above, on the slope, was an open-walled bamboo restaurant suspended over the lake. I looked beyond the restaurant and saw the red-tiled Spanish roof and white buildings of the hotel where we would be staying. The tiles ascended perfectly with the slope of the mountain. I took a deep breath and smelled tamales, spices, and beans. My mouth watered.

"This place is...this place is...perfect," I said, instantly falling in love with the whole scene. A feeling of adventure permeated every cell of my being.

Most of us are busy gambling on the most dangerous risk of all—living our whole life not doing what we want on the bet that we can buy the freedom to do it later.

Aligning the Condor and Eagle

San Marcos, December 22, 2010

One of your inalienable rights as a human being should be to receive a mysteriously useful omen every day of your life.

—Rob Brezsny

The burning rays of the sun were abusing the integrity of our white skin. The sight of the graceful carriage of women balancing crates of firewood on their heads kept my thoughts from dwelling on the oppressive temperature.

Cole, Colton, and I walked along a cracked stone path on our way into town. There was a little asphalt hill atop the town overlooking the lake, and so we made our way a few hundred feet into the village. The town was small--a mix between a tropical, spiritual paradise and an abused, poverty-stricken town. It told stories of exploitation in the old cracked buildings, tin shacks, and littered storm drains.

There was one main asphalt road, which ran parallel to the lake. Every twenty yards or so there was a narrow stone alleyway that journeyed perpendicular to the asphalt road, toward the lake. Eventually we turned down a similar path fastened with fresh coffee trees. A middle-aged man rested in a crunched-over position against a rock that caressed the fence of the orchards.

His face was lined in dried blood, his nose crooked, his clothes filthy. His mocha cheeks were sunken. His skin was beat up from too many unsheltered days in the sun. He slurred his words either from dehydration or drunkenness and asked us for money. We gave him what we could spare. He smiled and his spirit spoke without words.

We blessed him and kept on walking. I reflected on how alive I felt knowing that we come into this world with nothing and leave with nothing, so the only thing worth doing is giving. An orange hummingbird, or so it seemed to be, caught my eye. I smiled at the small bird, which was doing exactly that—offering its song freely to me.

We continued through the town in search of local food. I traced my hand along the wooden carvings of animals on the bamboo gates of little one-story shops. Shop after shop lined the hundred-yard path, with the exception of an occasional grassy, profusely littered, area.

While we walked, I admired the four-foot-wide stone path. Locals sat outside their shops; a few stared at us, but others smiled at my Bob Marley T-shirt. Some shops sold baked goods, others were little corner stores with water, and some were restaurants with a few tables.

The aroma of freshly baked banana bread intensified with each step we took. Moments later we crossed paths with an old woman who waved us off the asphalt road and into her small adobe restaurant: *Los Abrazos*—the hugs. I looked at the structure, which reminded me of some sort of Native adobe home I'd seen in a cartoon—perfectly red, rounded like a dome, covered with stone statues.

Her smile persuaded us to enter. Her temples were gray and complemented her midnight black hair. Her warm hands were pleasant to the touch, as she greeted each of us into the twenty-by-twenty-foot room.

The floor was concrete, with a few cracks that circled through the simple but elegant room. It was covered in a few red, yellow, and purple handmade floor mats. Three or four circular booths sat below wall carvings of Mayan warriors. We sat at the table nearest the small kitchen and were served cups of water. I placed my hands on the stone table and looked up, noticing the dark-red wooden beams from which hung a few candle lanterns.

Two chiseled-stone fire pits were angled in the far corners of the room, away from us. A massive stone carving of a condor rested above one fireplace, and an eagle above the other. Incense burned near them. The woman, whose name was Antonia, explained to us how she flame-cooked the meals in the pits.

Gentle sounds of children playing ball outside drifted through the cracks in the walls. We all watched her spark the fireplace with old palm fronds. When she was finished, my brother held up the menu and pointed to what looked like an advertisement. He asked Antonia in his best Spanish if she personally knew the shaman who was being showcased on the back of the menu.

She nodded her head and replied. "My son, Fernando! I can get him right after I put your food on! He is a healer. He has lived that kind of life since he was a small child and uses no drugs."

Hearing that a shaman was so close at hand, I laughed water through my nose. Life had brought us exactly what we wanted. I looked at my fingers as if they were magic wands, granting my every wish. I thought to just months earlier, when I held a vision of meeting a shaman. I was relieved to know that what I'd read about creating our dreams was true. Cole, Colton, and I exchanged knowing glances.

After lunch, Fernando Oxlaj glided through the doorway like high-altitude air. His slender frame suggested he had some rare power to go days without food and instead could live off the love within his own heartbeat. He was beardless, with chocolate eyes more inviting than Hershey's Kisses, and he had a smile that could propel the dust off of anyone. He was about twenty-seven years old, but he wasn't exactly sure because he had stopped counting long ago.

I studied the shaman's movements closely. His bare feet were stationed firmly on the ground, as if he were receiving power through the soles of them. His wisdom-edged chin gave him a peculiar nobility. He was dressed in torn beige cargo pants and a plain undersized orange crewneck T-shirt. I debated whether or not the sun rose at his command.

Thanking Antonia for the delicious food, we promised we'd return soon and followed Fernando out. As we walked onto the main road of town, I watched the mini silver taxis, tut-tuts, glint in the sun. Fernando led us through the middle of the town square. We walked down a concrete stairway of fifteen or so steps that led off the main road in town. There we found a few wooden stores and restaurants. We passed the local basketball court on the left. It was small and overcrowded, but it had a lot of character with its colorful wooden stands.

There was a brown stone planter with a large overhanging tree in the center of the square. Its green and brown leaves fluttered onto the gray concrete. Finding it unusually interesting that the asphalt was laced with cracks, yet still held together, I was reminded that even through our imperfections and egoism, we are still complete. I smiled at a few people who sat against the plant holder. They looked at us like we were special because we were walking with Fernando. A few wooden shacks on the right that sold tacos caught my eye. Aromas of fresh tortillas, coriander, pineapple, and coconut dangled in space.

"Please, let us continue to my home," Fernando whispered, as if a loud voice could disturb the fragrances that were suspended in the gentle breeze.

I was in awe of life by this moment. I had created *exactly* what I had wanted, but I didn't know what was next. I took a couple of breaths and wiped my sweaty palms on my pants. We turned off the main road onto a tree-lined walkway and went some twenty yards in single file. After a few moments, we turned off the stone path and onto a dirt path in the coffee fields. Thousands of coffee beans and green leaves carpeted the ground.

Fernando spoke again in Spanish, which my companions readily translated for me. "Many weeks ago I had a dream that three white men would arrive in my village. You look different than you did in my vision..." Fernando paused to laugh, his white teeth gleaming in the sunlight. "You see, imagination creates our world and determines the future, not intellect."

It was then that we approached a head-high wooden gate. There were a few stone steps that led through the gate and into his yard. We walked toward his concrete house with its black wooden doorframes. Just to the side of the home was an outhouse with no running water. After I used the restroom, I took shade under the lone coffee tree in the yard. And while my brother and Fernando spoke in Spanish, I made my acquaintance by a doghouse where Fernando's yellow Lab, Yesse, lived.

After Cole and Fernando spoke for a moment, we entered his home by climbing three wooden steps. I was careful to duck my head to fit through the small doorway. The space was just large enough to accommodate the four of us—Cole, Colton, Fernando, and me. No larger than the average-sized American bedroom, the home was just a single, windowless room with a loft. I could reach up and touch the ceiling if I tried. Even still, the space was drenched in subliminal power. The white concrete walls were splattered with small rosebud-sized cracks of wisdom, and paintings of Mayan's dancing in the sun hung from the wooden frames of the roof.

A few other paintings of Mayan gods and one of an aerial view of Lake Atitlan decorated the other walls. A large, red wooden rocking chair rested in one corner and a bamboo chair in another. A massive hiking stick resembling a wizard's shaft rested against it. In the back, a few wooden steps led up to the loft, which held Fernando's bed. Near the door, bundles of incense sticks sat atop a white table that stretched across the whole wall. Four bamboo meditation mats rested on the red concrete floor, forming a circle. At the center was a small altar holding an incense burner, three orange candles, and decorative green flowers.

A few pieces of paper were stacked neatly on the desk. Later, I'd discover that those papers were the blueprint for an orphanage we would later raise money to build. Fernando had known psychically that we would be along soon and had already started planning.

I quit looking around the room and watched Fernando read our energy. Clearly he was a man of nature. Even the birds' songs seemed to silence when he spoke—as if he told them his secrets or they told him theirs. He tossed an incense wrapper in a brass-colored trashcan beneath the desk. Then he began speaking so rapidly that Cole was the only one who could follow. Even then he didn't fully understand everything Fernando said because his main language was Mayan, not Spanish. Still, Cole assured Colton and me that sweet experiences awaited us over the next two weeks. *This* was the shaman we had been looking for.

"He told me he was going to read our minds, without drugs, one at a time, or something really wild," Cole said. "Who wants to go first?"

I declined the invitation, looking down at the cracked floor. I felt excited but also uneasy. My mind raced. I felt that if I waited, I would be calmer.

Colton ended up going first. We walked out of the room. Fernando closed the door behind us. My brother and I sat in two red plastic chairs by the doghouse. Cole told me I could go next. I watched him pull his black hood over his head and get into a meditative trance by focusing on his breath. I could hear a man and woman murmuring in hushed tones from down the walkway. Yesse, Fernando's dog, came out of his house and walked into the coffee fields toward the voices.

The sun was still hot but was beginning to droop down the mountains for a good night's sleep. Watching the shadowy shapes of the trees beyond the fence, I sat straight with my eyes closed—practicing focusing on my breath and relaxing.

Perhaps thousands of moments had passed before the wooden door flung open. Colton emerged. He looked unusually white, as if he'd just guzzled a liter of tequila and the effects were slamming him all at once, which was bizarre because Fernando told us more than once that he didn't use any drugs.

"What happened?" I immediately questioned without mindfulness.

Colton said nothing, only nodding his head. I wondered if his experience had been even more powerful than we had imagined it would be. Before he walked down the steps and out into the coffee fields, he turned to me and said, "Relax, Jake, or else you'll miss what Fernando's going to say." He could tell I was a bit uptight and nervous about what would happen in there.

Upon entering, I saw that Fernando had changed into his Mayan attire; a magical blue-and-white short-sleeve shirt woven from cloth. Brown beads stretched across the shirt. It seemed to hold both the sky and the clouds in each stitch. Blue lines zig-zagged up the sides of the mostly white shirt. There were a few faint designs of the sun on his stomach area. The rays traveled up the shirt. His pants were shimmering white cloth, matching the base color of his shirt. He still wore no shoes.

He instructed me to kneel on the mat in the center of the room. He lit a few yellow candles and sage-filled incense. Then, so that I would fully understand his message, he called Cole in to join us so that he could translate everything.

We sat in a triangle, each on a bamboo mat. I watched the incense smoke wander around the room like weightless leaves in the breeze. The cracked walls of the room made me feel wiser than I was. Then Fernando asked me to close my eyes.

I felt free to be myself. I had no idea that my "self" was about to shatter into a million pieces like broken glass.

Even through our imperfections and egoism, we are still complete.

A Miracle

San Marcos, December 22, 2010

I have never had the faintest reason since to change my views on psychical and spiritual phenomena, for which there is no foundation. The belief in these is the natural outgrowth of intellectual development.
—Nikola Tesla

Silence.

A warm hand was on my head. "Abre tus ojos! Abre tus ojos!" Open your eyes!

Fernando's words etched into my soul like the carpenter's chisel that bites into naked wood. The small room was dimly lit by candlelight. The musty odor of waterlogged cinderblock beams mingling with the incense created a unique orchestra for the senses. My beliefs about what's possible were about to crack like the old walls in the room.

I sat with my legs tucked neatly under what felt like the weight of the world. My eyes locked on to a man who looked very different from the Fernando I'd seen minutes before. His aura seemed purer, brighter. It appeared to me that he was almost like a superhero. He gazed deeply into my blue eyes with a steel-minded stare. It drew me closer like a magnet. I looked at his wizard's shaft and away from his eyes because I was afraid to focus. It occurred to me then that I was thinking too much, analyzing what was happening. As a result I concentrated on the whites of his eyes. Soon thereafter, I found myself inside them.

He held my right wrist in one hand as if it were a hot pan. His energy gave rise to a range of intense emotions. On some indescribable level, I felt enlightened by his presence. My entire body pulsated with energy. And while I can't fully articulate what happened next, my understanding of life changed instantly—forever, in that single moment. When God looks into your soul, it is as if you are looking into a mirror. If you look long enough you can't recognize anything you see; that face you see is not yours. Essentially, Fernando had channeled a meeting between God and me—although he would never label the experience with the orthodox parlance I use here. I do not know how long this event transpired. There is no concept of time when you are one with God, when you become God. And by *God*, I don't mean a man in the sky who judges us. I mean a thing, a force, the infinite source, spirit, All-That-Is. It's the love that permeates every cell of *everything* on this planet; a vibration that is conducted in our hearts.

I do not wish to change anyone's chosen stance on God or the essence of who they are. Our beliefs are our own free will and life fully supports us no matter what. And in case you were wondering about my sanity— *my mom did too*—I was fully conscious, sober, and awake during this meeting. This was truly a conduit for dialogue with the soul.

Cole translated everything Fernando said. He said he would tell me things about myself that I didn't think it would be possible for him to know. I felt like I was part of some mysterious fairy tale that I didn't yet understand but would in the future. He told me to relax and relayed how problems from my childhood had resulted in deep-seated anger that led me to abuse alcohol. "It led you to many threatening accidents," he said, nodding from a place of understanding. "You mustn't regret the mistakes you've made. *Current decisions equal destiny*."

I nodded in agreement, acknowledging that if we wish to change, we must do it with our current actions and thoughts. I took deep breaths. Tears slowly filled my eyes while I thought of my past. My heart zinged with gratitude that I had finally stopped "learning" and started "living."

Fernando continued to tell me, through my brother, what I knew but had trouble admitting: that alcohol shifted me away from the peaceful, creative, and contemplative sides of myself. I knew it hindered my perception of reality and had gotten me into a lot of trouble.

"Over the last two years you have been awakening to another part of yourself," Fernando said, while continuing to hold a hand on my head. He stared into my eyes. "Remember, the past is an illusion. The only thing that is important is your life at this moment. We are like onions. You lived the tough flavorless layers of yourself in your early years when you had your car accident. Now you are opening to who you really are."

The world around me froze, and I broke out in a sweat. Tears began streaming from my eyes. Fernando took a step back. I hadn't believed anyone could actually know someone else's mind with such flawless accuracy. The shaman paused to let me catch my breath, and my mind traveled to years past when I was too scared to admit to myself that partying wasn't helping me. My tears came down even harder as an answer to the question that had been haunting me since the night of my accident was finally answered. I finally knew why I didn't die in the car wreck. I was alive to tell of my transformation. My body shook wildly as a result of this realization, as if I was having that seizure I'd daydreamed about back in economics class.

Fernando stepped toward my now kneeling body once again. His bare feet made no noise on the floor while he walked. He placed his warm hands on my head before saying I must breathe very deep and long. His face was stern. He said a fire cannot burn by its past ashes, only by new wood and fuel. New actions, thoughts, and perceptions are our fuel.

"You are the fire. Now, you must burn, until you are living with meaning." He paused and looked through his mind for more wisdom. "We are entering the Age of Great Remembrance, where many will recall their true nature and powers. The Age of Great Forgetting is almost finished for humanity. Use your creative abilities to travel the world and share what you know in order to help the people...." He stopped and looked at me with a slight smile. "We are in debt to the world that has raised us. The only way anyone we can repay is by making people smile each day." His smirk expanded with a giggle. "All of our sorrows are forgotten the moment we smile."

I nodded and tasted the tears dribbling down my face. My brother sat adjacent to me, cross-legged, his expression unrevealing.

"Don't forget to meditate before sunrise each day," Fernando said. "Don't worry how your form is. Real meditation is not about mastering techniques; it's about letting go," he spoke slowly and often put his hand to his chin to think. "It can be lying down, sitting up, eyes closed or open. It can be a visualization of the future; it can be a thought-free time where the inner batteries are recharged. There is no right way, just focus on your breath."

He finished talking and placed his hands over his heart. He motioned for me to stand up. He hugged me. I cried and my body shook. When I regained my composure, Fernando put his arms around my shoulders and looked into my eyes. It was as if he was telling me I would be okay, that he would watch over me while I traveled the world.

I took a few steps toward the door, and then my brother reached his arms open for a hug. We held each other tightly for a moment, and then I left to head back to Hotel Jivana alone.

When I got into the coffee field, I picked a few fallen Kona berries and sucked the sugar out of them. I didn't encounter many people on my five-minute walk back to the hotel. That was probably a good thing, as my eyes were red from crying. The tears were largely because I realized that my experience with Fernando had taken me to a crossroads of existence. And at this crossroads I had for the first time taken the road less traveled. My only other option had been to continue the way I'd come, on the road where the lane dividers are painted with society's beliefs about *who we are* and *what reality is*. But what fun is it to live by another's standard—to journey a road if we know where it leads?

When I got back to the balcony of the hotel room, I smiled, feeling free, as I hadn't a clue where this new road would take me. Even the bedsheets felt different when I rolled in them that night. This was because I did not perceive my experience with the prejudices of yesterday, only with the innocence of the moment. I listened to nature's night sounds sing through the window. Only years ago I had been confused and frustrated. Now I rested in bed, knowing I had found my reason for living, finally realizing that heaven is both over our heads and below our feet.

**A fire cannot burn by its past ashes,
only by new wood and fuel. New actions,
thoughts, and perceptions are our fuel.
You are the fire. Now, you must burn,
until you are living with meaning.**

Give Up the Good, Receive Greatness

San Pedro, December 23, 2010

You can only lose what you cling to.

—Buddha

Rainbows in my hourglass say all the hours in the past were meaningful. Sitting in the sun with a mind full of dreams, out of space and time, I'll see where they lead.

Dawn.

For months before I'd left on this trip I'd felt an intuitive calling to Byron Bay, Australia, because it is said to be a mecca for travelers seeking more than just the ordinary limits of life. Moreover, I saw it as a hop, skip, and a jump from Asia. Thusly, I decided that morning for sure that I would go there next when Cole and Colton had to return home for work.

After I was sure of my choice, I dangled my feet over the brick balcony, gazing into the empty space and visualizing the place I intended to be in the near future. I wanted to jump off the balcony and build my wings in the air…a voice within cautioned me: *Take off from the ground, not the roof.*

I listened.

The lake began to reflect the first sunrays of the day like a mirror. A few birds played with one another just overhead. There was only one cloud in the sky, resembling an angel's halo; it was suspended over the tallest of the three volcanoes. I snapped a picture, not knowing at the time that it would one day grace the cover of this book.

Time strode on with particular regularity, at exactly the same velocity as the previous seconds. My entire nineteen years I had heard and believed the cliché "time is money." Yet while I sat pondering the ripples of the lake, I couldn't help but ask, "If there's no proof that time really exists, does that mean money is an illusion too?"

Then, time's reel of moments flashed forward some thousands of instances while Cole, Colton, and I boated across the lake to the neighboring town of San Pedro in order to use the ATM.

"How much for your shirt?" a man's voice called to me from the front of the ten-person boat. I laughed, giving myself time to contemplate the voices in my head. The first voice said, *No way man, it's a brand-new shirt and it's my favorite. Sorry!* The second said, *Those who give will receive. We are here to share. This man probably has very little money to buy new shirts and besides, it was only ten dollars.* I found the second voice more reasonable.

Before my selfish side had time to strengthen its grasp, I stripped off the Bob Marley "Positive Day" shirt and tossed it to the twenty-year-old native, Poncho.

"It's free!" I said with a smile.

I was now shirtless. Because of this act of generosity, which was a new experience for me, I felt different as we skimmed toward the town. It was as if the fishermen peppering the lake were casting out the characteristics of my life that I no longer needed.

The sky was flawlessly blue—the volcanoes, green and unscathed by civilization. A few other taxi boats skimmed the lake slowly at a distance. I watched from afar. A few ducks bobbed at the center of the glassy surface. I watched the water, which had always been some sort of natural dream catcher for me, expanding my dreams and imaginings and putting them into reality. Then Poncho, who spoke with unusually fluent English from his days interacting with tourists, said, "To me, the colors of red, yellow, green, and black have meaning beyond what most people think of on this Bob Marley T-shirt. Yellow stands for the new earth, without the war, oppression, and greed that is associated with money and our social divisions of economics, skin color, and national borders." He smiled while I stared into the cool blue sky and imagined such a world.

"Green depicts the hope for change that keeps me fighting day after day. Red is the blood of truth that has been spilt from the murders of men like Gandhi, Martin Luther King, and many others. Lastly, black embodies the troubles that will always be there in life, but that strong hearts and minds will conquer day by day, moment by moment." He paused and looked at Colton, Cole, and me to be sure we were following. We urged him to continue.

"It is important to be strong because now we are moving toward a stable society, where finding and focusing on our passion is the primary objective. In doing so, we create an earth where people are offering their fullest inner value into the material world."

I nodded in acknowledgment. So did the others. Right then, we all knew that we were on the same wavelength about what life meant to us. Poncho smiled wide and invited us to walk around his village and meet his family. We accepted.

We skimmed through a small patch of brown reeds as we pulled up to the tiny wooden dock. Most locals sat by the boats at the docks and watched them pass by while they enjoyed the sun. Poncho had said that with the recent decline in tourism due to perceived danger, the jobs had decreased drastically.

"There used to be twice as many boats shipping the tourists across the lake only a few years ago," he said.

I sat silently the rest of the ride until we came to a wooden dock about as big as a sedan to which Poncho tied the boat. As we hopped off, I couldn't help but be enormously happy. Earlier in the day, Cole, Colton, and I had talked about wanting to meet a local who would show us his way of life. And here he was.

Poncho's physique was similar to Fernando's, but at five-six, he was a bit taller. In fact, he was probably one of the tallest in all of the villages. We followed him off the swaying wooden dock toward the main drag in town, which was on the hill only steps away. The streets were coursed with restaurants and shops of all types. As we walked along, a few locals approached us with backpacks full of cashews—a favorite nut of mine. I bought some for later.

We continued slowly uphill. Discarded carrots and greens nearly smothered the ancient cobblestone streets. Locals sat outside their shops, watching us. Compassionate, genuine smiles laced their faces as they welcomed us gringos to their land in a different fashion than they had the day before. Perhaps it was our association with Poncho that made us more welcome. Our native tongue might have been different from theirs, but the language of the heart is spoken not by speech but through the loving intention of wanting to understand one another.

Poncho guided us to a restaurant, but none of us were hungry, just thirsty. We all sat down at a table on a wooden balcony that overlooked the lake. I pondered the rainbow in my glass of water and noticed out of the corner of my eye that our new friend took a sip from his own cup every time he finished saying something.

Why our guide's drinking habit was significant to me, I wasn't sure, but it made me wonder about being watched and studied...by peaceful aliens. What would they think of us and of all the little details of our lives? My imagination continued with the "what-ifs"....For all I knew the little stars that moved in intelligent circles through the night were little motherships of distant humanoids who were studying our bizarre evolution. Perhaps they are entertained by the fact that we are celestial infants—*celestial* because we are a part of the universe and cosmos, but *infants* because we hadn't yet figured out a way to live in harmony with ourselves, each other, or our home rock.

A flurry of Mayan dresses caught my attention and my strange thoughts dissipated. A few women approached our table and asked us to buy ponchos. My brother got one. They thanked us and giggled flirtatiously before carrying on with their simple day.

"Please, may I take you to my home to meet my mother and father?" Poncho asked.

Pleased by the invitation, we all nodded and finished our water. Soon we were continuing up the hill, following behind Pablo and passing even more shops selling the same wares—ponchos, blankets, necklaces, beads, cashews, and water.

Leaving the commercial area, we journeyed into the narrow alleys of the concrete residential areas. They housed the locals in small tilt-ups, which are tiny tent-sized homes that appear to be balancing in the air only by chance. They were divided by woven cloth and chain-linked fences about five feet high. Walkways were narrow, and water dripped from overhanging moss, almost onto our heads. It was more or less set up like a maze—very thin walkways with houses piled in every direction. Local's watched us curiously. The blond head of a North American was probably a rare sight for them. However, we weren't the typical tourists with cameras and sport shirts, seemingly dressed from another world. We were just ordinary people looking for love, laughter, and answers to life.

"Aye, Brotha!" a shirtless man, about forty years young, shouted happily, waving his hands from a nearby curb. "Long hair, long life!"

I made a peace sign, put it to my heart and then out into the air, allowing the wind to carry the vibration to him.

Soon after, we approached Pablo's home; the locals eyed us from their concrete porches, most likely because they couldn't tell if they were actually seeing three white people walk through their alley or if their eyes were playing tricks on them.

"Aqui! Look here!" some of the children yelled to their friends like we were some special treat to share.

A waft of corn tortillas passed my nose. The scent led the three of us to a fence, where I gazed over to see a family cooking in a communal circle. My mind rewound to moments in my childhood when my family sat together, seemingly without a care in the world. Some say that every experience we have moving forward reminds us of one that has passed, and at that moment, I saw how true that could be.

A few moments later, Poncho led the three of us through the doorway into his home. A magenta-and-yellow woven blanket had been serving as the door. When he moved it away so that we could enter, my heart thumped wildly at the sight of his parents' sparkling eyes and the genuine warmth with which they welcomed us into their home. My inner child emerged. I'm not prone to labeling someone's parents as "cute" by any means, but they were just that. I knew if I ever had enough ambition to create my own "pictionary," I'd place a photo of them next to the word.

The house was relatively small at about 700 square feet. It was entirely concrete, including the kitchen. However, most of the walls were decorated in yellow, green, and purple woven cloths his mother had made. There were no windows—just lots of concrete. A small bathroom was in the back left corner, and a couple bedrooms were along the same wall.

Then I looked at his father, who had an impenetrable beard like Ernesto "Che" Guevara's (the late Latin revolutionary who advocated a global uprising to combat the woes of poverty and predatory capitalism, where a few profit at the expense of many). A few gray lines streaked down his father's face like lightning across midnight black facial hair, which suggested a wise character. His rhythmic breath made me imagine he had seen every sunrise in history

I turned to his mother and admired her thick beautiful eyebrows, which hung above her copper eyes. Her pink cheeks were etched with wrinkles, suggesting she'd spent much of her life laughing. Just as wine improves as it ages, so too had Poncho's parents, I mused. In hindsight, wine and his parents had a great resemblance, as both held the capacity to make one drunk off the consumption of their presence.

The room was fluttering with substance-less abundance. On the walls, paintings of the lake looked more like windows than canvases with finite edges. Hand-woven tablecloths and other products Pablo's mother had made to sell at the market were purposefully scattered on the counters. She ushered us to a table covered with her artistry. She sat down with Colton, Cole, Poncho, and me, but Poncho's father stood in an odd, off-center stance, as if he had plenty of pain in his legs and back for us all.

Then, waving his index finger like an orchestra conductor, Poncho began to tell us that his father couldn't sit for extended periods of time because he had been seriously injured in their civil war, which had begun in 1960 and only ended as recently as 1996. Poncho's father had been a member of the civilian revolution army, which was formed to protect the people of Guatemala. In 1954 the democratically elected government of Jacobo Arbenz was overthrown in a CIA-organized military operation. The new government that came into power slaughtered more than 200,000 innocent Guatemalans.

During the war, Poncho's father had been captured, and along with hundreds of others, marched into deserted land. They were ordered to dig massive holes in the ground and were forced inside them under the relentless sun for two weeks. Afterward, they were imprisoned for two years before finally being released.

The most amazing part, as Poncho explained, was that his father had forgiven his captors. This was because he understood that forgiveness sets us free. Poncho said that his father had spent many years very angry, but now that he had let it go, he had been happier than ever.

"We believe that whether you were here to experience it or you weren't born yet," Poncho said as his tale was drawing to a close, "you are still a child of war. In our age, we're all children of war. We fight malnourishment, disease, poverty, and greed every day as one collective human race."

He grew quiet, and a poem flew into my head: "*Sitting on the horizon looking at the sun, a mind full of questions, I'm not the only one. Many ways, many views, without change, we all lose. Mirror, mirror, in the sky, could you tell me why no one cares or dares to speak their mind?*"

Colton, Cole, and I absorbed this history lesson and speech without reply. I was amazed. As a result, I twiddled my thumbs a bit and looked around at Poncho's mother's artwork.

"What does forgiveness mean to your family, Poncho?" I asked finally.

Poncho smiled and looked through his mind while he placed a hand on his dad's shoulder. He spoke to him in Spanish, telling him what I had asked.

"Forgiveness is alchemy of the soul in which the feeling of possibility returns to the human spirit."

I smiled and said nothing. Poncho knew I had no fitting response besides a "thank you." My brother got up and grabbed a few tablecloths to purchase from Poncho's mom. Colton did the same. A few minutes later we hugged them good-bye and left.

When we departed, I inched down the patio stairs, attempting to stuff the cardinal virtue of forgiveness I'd learned into my heart. I spotted the friendly stares of the local children. Having forgotten to watch my step, I hit the stones below with a dense thud and collapsed like a tall tree. Knowing I wasn't injured, Colton and Cole laughed uncontrollably. Unhurt but embarrassed, I peeled my skin off the ground pound by pound.

"You know you have to use your feet when you walk, brotha?" an English-speaking boy joked to me.

I gave him a smile. With tears of humor in my eyes, I knew with almost fatalistic certainty of the facts, that with my head in the clouds, I had been pushed over by the air.

I wiped the dust off, and followed the backs of Poncho, Cole, and Colton until I caught up. Poncho escorted us back through the same alley toward a soccer field where the children and young adults played their league games. There was a beautiful view, as it was on the base of a lush green side of the San Pedro volcano.

A chain-link fence sectioned off the area. They had two goals without nets and a fairly large field of dirt littered with rocks and weeds. It bore little resemblance to what I had grown accustomed to. I don't think the ten children even noticed as they happily paraded barefoot around the field. A half-flat ball missing much of its leather proudly danced through the air. The kids hooted and ran free, while the birds watched from above.

"We play league games every other day," Poncho explained. "It's how I get away from life. Sure, a stadium with real grass and goals would be ideal, but we don't know any better, so it doesn't affect us. Instead of longing for what we don't have, we love all that we do have. Knowing our thankfulness will bring us more of what we love, because it's how the world works. Appreciate to receive!"

My brother, our friend, and I exchanged smiles of gratitude. I slid off my sandals to fit in better. Poncho shouted with joy when one of the littlest guys scored. We took seats on the ground against a few old tree stumps that were almost like stadium stands.

The sun was starting to set, which triggered our farewells to Poncho for the day. While my mind had been busy flipping around during our visit, I had lost all track of time. So while we walked through town, I was hardly aware that the starving dusk had eaten all but a sliver of the golden sun. When we reached the docks, we jumped onto the boat for the five-minute ride back to San Marcos. I relaxed into the view of the moon's nightly inauguration as chaperone over the darkness. My body tingled with a deep feeling of peace that was beyond anything I'd experienced.

Forgiveness is alchemy of the soul in which the feeling of possibility returns to the human spirit.

Transforming the World

San Marcos, Christmas Eve, 2010

When we give our energy to a different dream, the world is transformed. To create a new world, we must first create a new dream.

—John Perkins

"Do dogs like bones?" Fernando asked us, pointing to his dog, Yesse, curled up on a mat in the corner of the room.

Cole, Colton, and I all nodded from our place on the bamboo mats. I didn't know if he was messing with us, so I kept my eyes on the candle flame in the center of our sitting circle.

Fernando laughed loudly and slapped his white pants, playfully shoving the bamboo mat across the room. He took a deep breath and waved some incense smoke around.

"Dogs don't like bones," he said with a smile. "They settle for bones! Dogs like meat...What are you settling for in your life and dreams?" He looked right at me before moving to sit on the rocking chair a few feet away.

"The future is not a place you get to go; it's a place you get to create from your heart."

The morning was warm and so was the concrete floor, making it easier for me to relax my mind and just listen—without internal dialogue about things that may never happen. I took a deep breath and felt the cozy environment of the tiny home. Through the open door I listened to a few birds chirp. I yawned, thinking that the three of us awoke at five in the morning this Christmas Eve to meditate and speak with Fernando, something we had been doing before starting each day—just usually an hour or two later.

"And most people are very creative...they can usually discover many reasons why something can't be done."

Fernando rocked in his chair like a little kid. He whistled to Yesse, who went to lie next to him. I smiled at Cole and Colton, who sat across from me on their mats.

"Humans are streams whose sources are veiled," he said.

Sometimes it was easy to forget that Cole and Colton were translating, but Fernando was not speaking English. They continued to interpret for me, and I would reiterate the lesson: "Our purpose is buried within us behind our fear, and doubts. Finding our purpose is the only way we will transform the world. To find it, ask yourself, *What comes easy to me, but harder to other people?*"

Fernando's eyes searched his head for his next words. He rubbed his hands together as if conducting wisdom. I watched Yesse lick her paws and waited.

"There's an unwritten rule that we *all* aren't meant to live our dreams. Forget it! Once you can answer the previous question—*What comes easy to me, but harder to other people?*—then act as if your success is for certain. Doubt is what does the most damage."

Once translated, I repeated these words to myself, meeting Fernando's eyes to show him that I understood and that I was grateful for his time. He smiled.

He continued, "Now, the infamous Mayan calendar time of 2012 and beyond is about removing old masks about who you are and just being yourself."

I nodded. Cole and Colton were wearing grateful smiles.

"While this dream of life is being reimagined, it's important to remember—slippery is the slope that everyone has already climbed," Fernando said with a laugh as he watched Yesse walk out the door. "It's slippery because others' footprints have worn away the crevices you need to dig your feet into so that you may climb the peak. The view is best from the summit," he added. "Not from the resting point where everyone else watches the clouds pass." He stood up and went across the room to light more incense. "My brothers, sometimes we have to leave the trails, ignore the caution signs, and scale the mountain for the best view!" He let out a raucous laugh.

We laughed as well. Here we were in a concrete shack in the middle of the coffee fields beneath a plywood roof realizing that unless we intend to do something beyond what we know we can do, we rob ourselves of life's precious moments.

Then Fernando became a little more serious, and said in a hushed tone, "All of this...this process of risk taking to be unique, to be different, to have everlasting happiness—this is called the Cycle of Chance, and it is one of life's greatest gifts to humans. The cycle has three parts: commitment, action, reward. Make a *commitment* to be original, *act* with a bit of risk, and be *rewarded*."

I scratched my head and looked down at my mat. I breathed in the energy of the room to keep my spirit lifted. Fernando laughed and said that it was a good note to end on.

As we left, Fernando hugged each of us good-bye, telling us about his Christmas tradition to wake up at 2:00 am to exchange hugs (rather than physical presents) with his family. We wished him and his family well, and then he honored us with his hands in the prayer position as we left. We walked down the wooden steps into the fallen leaves and out into the coffee fields.

This process of risk taking to be unique, to be different, to have everlasting happiness—this is called the Cycle of Chance, and it is one of life's greatest gifts to humans. The cycle has three parts: commitment, action, reward. Make a commitment to be original, act with a bit of risk, and be rewarded!

Smile Please

San Marcos, Christmas Day, 2010

All people smile in the same language.
—Ancient Proverb

Dawn.

I scratched the dreams from my hair, rising up from my bed. The sun rose too and watched me watching it. The situation became a bit of a staring contest, and we were caught in limbo—until, at last, its beams blinded me.

Sitting beside Cole and Colton, I thought of what Fernando had said the day before: "Humans are streams whose sources are veiled." I could definitely feel the river of possibilities flooding my every thought and action. I itched to get out and greet the day. I threw on one of my Bob Marley T-shirts—from a collection that was quickly diminishing—and I left Cole and Colton behind to relax. Soon thereafter I learned one of the most important lessons of my travels: that our offers of friendship, laughter, and compassion speak louder than words and directly to the heart.

Spreading my mouth into the curve of all things jolly gave my teeth a chance to breathe, but it also showed a sincere offer of friendship. This is how I approached two young boys who were kicking a beat-up soccer ball in the asphalt alley near the local homes. It didn't bounce much, and when it would hit the ground, it hit with the *splat* of an orange smashing the cement. Its condition symbolized their poverty, and I had the desire to change that—all children should have a good, solid ball to play with.

Not many tourists hung around the alleyways in the village, so I inched near, making sure they saw me and wouldn't be alarmed by my presence. While I inspected the quarter mile or so of an old asphalt road, I watched locals walk in and out from the chain-link fences along the road—the front gates to their concrete lean-to homes.

I noticed that my Bob Marley T-shirt made the two kids smile. I stood about fifteen yards away with a grin on my face, not letting it fade, showing that I had come for friendship. My feet connected the third dot of a triangle for a game of passing the ball, just at the beginning of the asphalt street. Some moments later, the older boy slammed the ball in my direction. I kicked it up to myself and headed it to the other boy. The kids burst out with laughter at my antics, and I exploded with joy. It was good to be laughing with people I hadn't yet conversed with. It occurred to me that perhaps language had been designed to limit the voice of the heart and that maybe we would have all been better off being telepathic.

At exponential rates the ball skidded in my direction. I was quickly gaining respect as a friend, even though my performance was borderline atrocious. It was the most I'd laughed with anyone before even knowing their names. After we played for a while, the boys came over to introduce themselves. They spoke no English, but the language barrier made for more laughs as we struggled to understand one another. A few minutes later, when we decided we were better at playing than conversing, we went back to our game.

After some more time had passed I noticed that we had a group of spectators; several men, women, and children had gathered around on the asphalt. Some of the other kids joined the game, bringing along their own deflated balls. I was being booted balls by more kids than I could count. And I realized then, between dizzying outbursts of laughter, that besides being with my family, I couldn't imagine anything in the world that I would rather have been doing on Christmas Day. I was gaining respect for the Guatemalan culture and enjoyed submersing myself in it. The most profound Christmas present I had ever received was unity itself. I felt in accord with the flow of life and felt an awareness of the connection of all that exists. *Who needs Christmas lights,* I thought to myself, *when the hearts of my new friends gleam with truth.*

I had been concerned that I didn't speak the language before we'd arrived in Guatemala, but now I clearly understood how limiting words can be and how much more valuable a simple smile can be. I also knew that I could use this approach time and time again, especially if I saw a frowning face. An authentic smile reflects love, which has the power to override negative emotions. I also saw what appreciation for life was bringing me. The more I felt gratitude for the experiences I was having and the people I was meeting, the more I was being invited to enjoy new opportunities to further my understanding of the world and myself. Gratitude was my key to abundance.

I was sorry to leave my new friends behind, but I had agreed to meet Cole and Colton back at Hotel Jivana to eat cashews and watch the sun fall on our brick balcony. With our feet over the edge, we'd stay there for the rest of the night.

Christmas in Guatemala would become one of my fondest memories of the holiday: no presents, decorations, lights, trees, turkey, or ham. It was just us—just the lost boys, giving and receiving the gifts of our universe. I learned that day the truth of the old adage—*the best things in life are free.*

I clearly understood how limiting words can be and how much more valuable a simple smile can be. I also knew that I could use this approach time and time again, especially if I saw a frowning face. An authentic smile reflects love, which has the power to override negative emotions.

Creating Change—2012 & Beyond

San Marcos, January 7, 2011

> *You are more than a human being, much more. For within your heart is a place, a sacred place where the world can literally be remade.*
>
> —Drunvalo Melchizedek

On our last day in Guatemala, Cole, Colton, and I walked down to Fernando's place. We had spent the past ten days meditating and speaking with Fernando. In the afternoons, we sat around the lake and talked with locals, especially the kids.

When we arrived at the shaman's house, a few of the locals were standing around in his yard. Fernando's few belongings were outside—his mattress, his bamboo chair, his rocking chair, even his mattress.

"My brothers, it's great to see you!" he said with a big smile.

In response to our unspoken question about what was going on, he explained to us, "I'm giving away my things to those in need." He let this sink in a bit, and then tacked on: "Teach through action." (The profound part of his messages often came when least expected.)

His words had left me scratching my head. I realized then that he wasn't giving away *extra* belongings. He was giving away things that he used every day. Here was a man living in complete inequity still freely offering all he owned. My knees grew wobbly. Fernando's words and actions continued to spark within me a clear knowing that we *can* do *anything* if we believe. The shaman wasn't concerned with lack because he had faith that all of his needs would be met.

"I'm sorry we cannot meditate right now. Come back this afternoon when all this is cleared away," he told us, and turned his attention back to the men in the yard.

We wandered through the coffee fields all the way to Los Abrazos. There we could drink *mate* tea at his mother's adobe restaurant. When we arrived, a stray dog welcomed us by cordially decorating the stone walkway with its feces. We stepped around it and walked inside. There we saw about ten local children in the small room.

"We are having a music festival for the morning to show our appreciation for all we have in life!" one boy said with innocence that stirred away the rancidity of the dog's "business."

It was only a matter of moments before bunches of kids with battered drums, guitars, and flutes were running to us. I picked one up by his dirty and undersized shirt. And it was then that Evelyn, Fernando's niece, smiled at me. Her two front teeth had grown in big, as adult teeth, while the rest were very small baby ones. She stared past my white skin and beyond my eyes with this innocence that had me caught between two universes, one of childlike youth and one of solemn maturity. My cells vibrated at their very core, propelling me into the childlike universe. There I could not move until the music began spiraling, banging on my very heart. Then both my feet began moving side to side. My hips did too. While I moved about, I inspected the eagle and condor fireplaces and the Mayan sculptures a bit more closely. A sign in English block letters caught my eye. It was hanging on some crate wood just above the kitchen, adjacent to our table. I stopped dancing and read it aloud:

The Story of the Condor and the Eagle

The ancient prophecies of the Maya, Inca, and Hopi declare now is the time for the Eagle of the North and the Condor of the South to fly together in the same skies. Since Cortes landed over 500 years ago, the Eagle has dominated through material and technological strength. In order to save the world, we need the ancient wisdom and heart-centered energy of the Condor to balance the Eagle energy. This is happening now! Los Abrazos (the hugs) is an expression of this desired unity.

As I stood there reading it again and again, the music began to die down. I took a seat at an empty table where Antonia had placed tea for us. I sat in the chair looking at the sign, realizing that I was alive in one of the greatest times in human history, as this generation will change the world! All ancient culture had even prophesized about it! While I reflected in my inspiration, Cole and Colton read the sign.

The three of us spoke briefly of its profundity and then decided to go back to Fernando's and talk on the way. We hugged everyone good-bye and headed out, leaping over dog poop as we did so.

When we arrived back at Fernando's place, no one was inside. We sat on the steps outside his brown gate. I took a deep breath, reveling in the freedom of the air. While we waited, I ate Kona berries off the coffee trees, spitting the seeds into the piles of colorful leaves on the ground.

The sky was clear like our minds. We sat quietly together in meditation. A few stray dogs joined us from time to time, only to wander away through the trees. After about an hour, Fernando approached on the dirt path and said that he had been visiting his father in the hospital. He explained that his father had been a very serious alcoholic for his entire life and saw it as the only way to escape the miseries of inequity. Fernando further explained that although his father was never around for him as a child, he had taught him an important lesson: alcohol inhibits our capacity to love family.

I nodded in complete agreement, having experienced a similar truth in my own life.

"If every alcoholic gave their money for beer to a child without food," he said, motioning for us to join him through the gate and inside his home, "then nobody would be starving on our planet."

As we had on so many days previous to this one, the three of us knelt on the concrete floor of Fernando's home. The only difference was that this time there was less furniture—just four bamboo mats, paintings over the concrete walls, and the white desk in the far corner.

Fernando lit incense in the center of the circle. We calmed our bodies and minds. As he spoke, his voice sounded otherworldly—gentle yet firm. Though I could understand only parts of his sentences, the rhythmic vibration of his voice eased my mind. During these sessions, he often repeated lessons he had shared previously, but I always found some new insight.

"The entire water of the sea can't sink a ship unless it gets inside the ship. Similarly, the negativity of the world can't put you down unless you let it get inside of you." With that, he paused and gave each of us a serious, searching look.

I nodded in response, allowing his words to imprint onto my memory so that I would always be able to recall them when I was sharing my lessons with the Western world.

"A spider begins her web slowly, making progress every day. Soon she builds her masterpiece and stabilizes her life. Stay patient with dreams," he added.

The room was silent. The space was filled with an unknown element that permitted me to dream freely. I remembered myself as a creator of my life. Part of me embraced my power. The other part only wanted to accept responsibility when life was going my way. Nonetheless, I knew I needed to stay aware of my power at all times so that the outside world would not make my decisions for me.

Fernando reminded us often that it all comes down to our free will: Free will is a double-edged sword. A person either hinders their well-being, if they are unaware of their behavioral patterns, or brings to life that which benefits their well-being if they are aware of their patterns. My patterns were clear to me now. We spent a few more moments in silence, then Fernando put down his wooden shaft and thanked us for allowing him to share his particular Mayan tradition's wisdom with us, which is called *Quiché*. The word itself means many trees, and the tradition dates back beyond the tenth century. We thanked him for sharing these lessons with us, and then soaked up the last of our time with this insightful being as he continued speaking.

"'Too many people live within unhappy circumstances but will not take the initiative to change their situation, because they are unaware of their power to do so," he said. "Truly being yourself is more than enough to transform the planet," he reminded us again. "Whenever you have trouble in the busyness of the world, stop and look within. You'll find the answers that will continue to guide you. It's those who don't have a foundation in the spiritual world and cannot let go of the old way of life that won't endure the coming world shifts. Yet there is no end to our being; we are endless and eternal."

Then Fernando summed up his teachings by telling us that in 2012 and beyond, humanity must firmly embrace the rebirth of all people through the actions of love and generosity. Rebirth is not an act of changing what is natural, he explained, but utilizing our natural power to make a difference. It's rebirth because it can help the people to rise up from the well in which they are drowning. It's an internal process, a rebirth of heart, culminating in a social rebirth as every heart is born anew. All humans must work together to establish a world with a rebirth of human conscience. The world as a whole cannot wait. We must be the change now, or we will experience our own self-destruction.

If we cannot let go of our outdated ways of life, I realized, *our minds really will experience their own demise. It is he who wants the world to remain as it is who does not want it to remain at all.*

Fernando's smile lit up the dark room. When he finished speaking, I felt the power surging through me. I knew it would guide me as I continued my journey across the world. My life felt complete, although it was just now unfolding.

Our journey in these parts had come to an end for now, and we hugged Fernando good-bye. I was certain I'd see him again, though. Plus, the wisdom he offered so freely for these few weeks would always be readily available in my heart.

We went back to our place along the main road in town to gather our bags. I took a last look at the lake from the brick balcony—saying farewell to the bird kingdom that hummed above the palm trees alongside the grassy shoreline. On the way back to the town center, we talked about the highlights of our experiences.

"I'm most grateful to see how others live around the world…I don't know if I can ever complain again," Colton said energetically, "after knowing that most children don't even have an extra pair of clothes, yet they still smile."

Bags in hand, we kicked rocks while we walked along the road back into the town center. "I'll always remember Poncho's father," I said. "It's—it's—it's so hard to believe that someone could be thrown into a hole in the ground for two weeks and still forgive!"

My brother laughed and playfully told me he forgave me for when I used to bite my own arm as a kid and then tell my parents that he did it!

"I guess Poncho's father's story can even teach me to forgive myself for being such a brat when we were younger," I said to my brother.

He laughed.

I poked my brother a few times in the chest like I did when we were younger, and then I asked, "What will always stick in your memory?"

"How one person, Fernando, could keep the hopes alive for hundreds of people in his village--doing it all without running water or electricity!"

"Yeah," Colton said, "Yeah!" as he took a few steps ahead of us and reached the children who were waiting for us at the wooden foodstand by the bus stop. I looked over at my brother and ahead to my friend. I would be sad to part ways with them, but I knew, like me, they would be guided to where they needed to be next. As for me, I was headed to Australia.

The three of us sat on the asphalt surrounded by the group of children we'd spent much time with throughout our stay. Their eyes were filled with sorrow for our departure.

"Why are you leaving us? When will you return? Don't you know you are like family to us?" Evelyn, Fernando's niece, said, as she clung to my arm.

I smiled at her, holding her hand, telling her that I would return.

I pulled out my camera to catch some pictures of these kids who had had such a profound impact on my life in such a short time. Eyes coveting the camera as if it were a bag of candy, they jumped into poses, throwing up peace and hang-loose signs. They spat out their tongues and climbed atop one another. They ran to the little wooden corner store and grabbed the food signs, hanging them on their bodies for some unknown reason.

I let them hold the camera, and within minutes they were taking photos at a record pace. One, two, thirty, seventy, three hundred. Within an hour, the memory card on my camera was full. They paraded around the center of town like they'd found the elixir of life: a simple digital camera.

The blue bus of departing sorrow had finally arrived. The kids grabbed our bags and chauffeured us onto the tin can with wheels. Most of the town watched us, and before climbing aboard, I caught a glimpse of Fernando on the minitaxi ahead. His smile took me to another place where his golden aura shone vibrantly. I absorbed the power he radiated and stored it away for future use. Once settled in my seat, I rolled down the window. Evelyn practically tried to climb inside when I reached my hand to her. She grabbed on to it.

"Promise to return as soon as you can, because we will miss you!" she said.

I nodded my head, and as the wheels began to turn, the grasp of her innocent hand became lost to me. Tears strolled down her cheeks, and the bus rolled away.

In 2012 and beyond, humanity must firmly embrace the rebirth of all people through the actions of love and generosity. Rebirth is not an act of changing what is natural, but utilizing our natural power to make a difference. It's an internal process, a rebirth of heart, culminating in a social rebirth as every heart is born anew.

Part Three

Australia: Ask and Receive

I Am...

Gold Coast, January 11, 2011

> *Then Jesus told them, "I tell you the truth, if you have faith and don't doubt, you can do things like this and much more. You can even say to this mountain, May you be lifted up and thrown into the sea, and it will happen."*
>
> —Matthew 21:21–22

Just before the plane had landed in Coolangatta, Australia, I asked the woman sitting beside me if she knew anywhere to stay. She just stared at me, probably wondering whether or not I was just plain stupid. I had no maps, I knew nobody, and I had pronounced the name of the town wrong. After correcting my pronunciation, she told me she couldn't help.

"The best adventure is the feared and unplanned one," I told her with a smirk as we exited the plane.

While walking I thought I heard her whisper to someone, "Yes, light does travel faster than sound. That is why that kid seemed bright until he spoke..."

I laughed.

I had washed up on the Gold Coast, home to some of the most beautiful surf beaches in the world. The small airport where we landed could only accommodate a few planes. Fortunately, it was just a quarter mile from the coast and I could see the ocean! The seashore was unblemished by building materials and stretched as far as my eyes could see.

I grabbed my backpack from the small baggage claim sometime around five o'clock. When I picked it up there was a television on with the news. I looked away quickly, as evening news is where they proceed with "good evening," and then tell you why it isn't. Then I aimlessly strode down the boardwalk, which separated the dense buildings from the white sand. I walked without the reservation of needing to be anywhere at any particular time. The contrast between the unblemished ocean and the buildings reminded me of Mission Beach, San Diego, where houses and hotels nestle against the sand. I began to wonder if the four building blocks of the universe were actually fire, water, concrete, and glass.

The sun was hot, perhaps too hot. I rubbed the sweat off my face with my white T-shirt and took a breath. It took me a moment to realize that I wasn't hallucinating when I saw the cars driving on the "wrong" side of the road. I smiled to myself because it reminded me that I was on the other side of the world.

The curb separating the boardwalk from the street was high. I climbed up, pretending to be a tightrope walker. It was a bit difficult to balance with my backpack, and I hadn't gone more than fifteen feet when a blue sedan full of beautiful women pulled over and hollered to me. The driver's blue eyes caught my attention; her smile was more radiant than the blaring sun. After I got out of her eyes, I told them I had no idea where I was headed. They laughed and offered me a quick lift to the Sands, a local hostel. The drive was too short. They told me that the Sands was the best beach around, and dropped me off. Unfortunate or not, I never saw them again. Oh, the woes of falling into someone's eyes without road signs to bring you back to reality....

The streets were narrow and had a small-town feel. Most of the structures were wooden. The main street, splattered with local businesses, led to a roundabout full of hundreds of white and yellow flowers. The hostel was white too, with wooden steps. I meandered in through the open door.

I asked the man at the front desk for a shared room. I watched his blue eyes search a binder. He was short, about five-six, with brown hair that was starting to grow as gray as his shirt. After booking me for a Greyhound bus at six in the morning to Byron Bay, he led me upstairs to a wooden bunkroom with three bunk beds. No one was staying with me for the night. I walked across the room and parted one of the heavy curtains, and a smile parted my face. Behind the curtain was a balcony overlooking the ocean.

I gladly flung my bag onto the second bunk and sorted through it. Then I inspected the fake plants in the corner. They looked dead. *Perhaps they haven't been watered,* I thought. Then I chucked at my own joke.

I felt grateful to be on the other side of the world to test the power of the human spirit. And from my bed I watched the sky out the window. I reveled in the fact that stars obliterate all the anxiety and fatigue one naturally feels when entering a foreign land without plans. In the morning I knew I'd be ready to test the validity of my newfound wisdom from Guatemala. Did I have the courage to stare the world straight in the eyes in this unfamiliar place with just a backpack and passport to my name? Was I looking for something outside myself that was within me? If I found that courage inside myself, then I'd know that I *really can* do anything. My heart beat with anticipation.

I closed my eyes. In my mind I held the image of meeting like minds. Imagination—which is often undeveloped in today's world—is the highest power of thought that we have, allowing us to bring miracles to life. Understanding how to use the creative right hemisphere of the brain helps thoughts materialize quicker. When our ability to visualize is developed into a strong tool, thoughts can begin to materialize instantly. This is illustrated by the ancient texts describing the seemingly miraculous actions of the spiritual masters. In today's modern world, we rely too much on the left hemisphere, which focuses on memorization and linear reasoning.

This being true, as I drifted into sleep, I was thankful that my father had taught me well while I practiced basketball as a child in my backyard: "By wholeheartedly believing in what doesn't yet exist, we make it so," he'd tell me.

Imagination—which is often undeveloped in today's world—is the highest power of thought that we have, allowing us to bring imaginative miracles to life. Understanding how to use the creative right hemisphere of the brain helps thoughts materialize quicker. When our ability to visualize is developed into a strong tool, thoughts can begin to materialize instantly. This is illustrated by the ancient texts describing the seemingly miraculous actions of the spiritual masters.

Allowing What's Meant to Be

Byron Bay, January 25, 2011

> *Asking is the beginning of receiving. Make sure you don't go to the ocean with a teaspoon. At least take a bucket so the kids won't laugh at you.*
>
> —Jim Rohn

The geckos did their daily push-ups on the hissing concrete. I hid from the tyrannical sun under a tree branch, admiring my bronzed tan. Feeling slightly disoriented from the heat that was far greater than Guatemala's, I closed the book I'd been leafing through: *Manifest Your Destiny* by Dr. Wayne Dyer. Then I wandered the windy dirt path through the campground with over a hundred tents to my mansion—a two-room tent flatteringly furnished. It was a free place to stay, a quarter mile off the coast of Byron Bay, circled around a marsh inlet from the ocean, with just a ten-dollar site fee, which I received from a Swiss friend—Armadeus. I met him when I first arrived in Byron Bay a week and a half earlier, just before he left to travel South America. He was a wise guy, about my age, and we had many talks about using our hearts to create our lives, but he was never around too much since he liked to go to the beach and meditate alone. Nonetheless, *I asked and I received.*

Bordering a wild sanctuary of a lush emerald forest around a two-hundred-foot-wide marsh, my temporary home stood proudly equipped with lanterns and mattresses, and a covered patio with chairs to capture the simplicity of the natural refuge. I listened to the foreign chants from rare birds. Attempting to understand their language brought me peace and purified my mind. And while I tranquilized on my stoop, three strangers approached. They told me they were from Israel—fresh out of a three-year army service. They were traveling Australia by camper van and had just purchased the tent beside mine.

I had never met any native Israelis before, and quite frankly, I didn't know what to expect. I waited for them to unpack their bags and have lunch. Excitement crept up through my spine. I had a feeling these three men would wash away any stereotypical preconceptions I had about Middle Easterners. I intuitively knew they had come to me as a manifestation of my intentions to interact with like-minded people, who were also looking for more than to just drink.

Furthermore, I still was feeling a bit too Westernized. I knew I wanted to be in Asia, a culture completely unknown to me. I hadn't firm plans as to when to head in such a direction, but while in my visualization, I imagined meeting someone who would steer me appropriately.

While I waited, my mind replayed the memories of my recent excursion as a homeless person while I was waiting for the tent to become available. I'd decided to store all my belongings with the former tent owner and venture off for three nights to live on the beach.

A little over a week ago, when I first arrived in Byron Bay, a small artsy town with mostly one-story wood buildings, I had been particularly struck by the plight of a homeless man. It was a burning hot day and he sat in the grass town square above the beach with severe sunburns, looking intensely dehydrated. I believed that he and other homeless people deserved more. For my whole life I never had to worry about where to sleep, what to eat, or what people would think about me if I had nothing. I realized that in order to gain a glimpse into how more than 200 million people live, I had to try my hand at homelessness.

Contrary to Western thought, I was comfortable and found it amusing when people passed by in the evenings and would discuss whether or not I was really sleeping in the sand, a few feet from the lapping water. During the days in town, walking alongside the small wooden shops, people stared at me with scorn, thinking I was homeless. Never before had I felt so judged. I was proud to be comfortable enough with myself to be able to step out of society like this. I knew that the only way to be content and significant was to be unique, because if we are thinking like others, then we aren't thinking at all.

Once, while rolling up the towels that I made home, I smiled at a man and his son as they walked the beach. They turned away. Ironically, I felt no disheartening feelings toward them. They felt pity for me, but I felt pity for them. They were judging me by their own standards of what they considered acceptable and had clearly decided that their way was superior.

Each night, in the natural bed of the coastline, I elected to sleep fewer hours than usual. The purple, red, and white stars that encompassed the sky took the place of dreams. Each morning, before sunrise, gravity's parachute pulled me back to the world, rubbing sleep from my eyes and dreams from my hair. It's an enlightening feeling to be the first on the shore for three consecutive days of sunrise. I stared into the sky amidst an hour of magic. Outbursts of yellow light crept over the water, firing questions into my stream of consciousness, such as "Who are you and why are you here?"

I stood silently in the grass above the beach on my last displaced morning, as a gray-haired man of skinny stature and a radiant aura approached. "What do you say on this beautiful day, young fella?"

"In comic strips, the person on the left speaks first. This life is one big joke, and you're on my left, I'd like you to tell me what you feel first, sir..."

He laughed while I debated if that was stupidest thing I'd ever said. "I've seen you each of the last three mornings and you're welcoming the day before me. No one ever does that...so let me get right to my questions. If I were to have a million dollars in my pocket right now to satisfy you forever, what would you do with your life? And when it's all said and done, will you have said more than you've done?"

Looking out at the ocean and smiling with gratitude that I had the opportunity to meet a man as interesting as he seemed to be, I spoke, "Well, I wouldn't trade anything for what I am doing right now..."

He continued in a soft but energetic voice while we stood on a grass hill above the beach. "It's funny, people have ideas of how we should live our lives, but none about their own." He reached his slender arm out for a handshake before he continued. "I'm the longtime preacher at the local church of full-loving consciousness and half-caring-about religious dogma. There, we follow St. Paul's words, 'Let this mind be in you, which was also in Christ Jesus: Who being in the form of God, thought it not robbery to be equal with God.'"

I laughed heavily, awaking anyone sleeping in nearby homes. It was silent after he, too, laughed. I put my bag on the ground and looked at the empty shore. I put my hand in my shoulder-length hair, finding it hard to believe how much sand was in it. I smiled and looked at the man.

After rubbing his hands together, he put one on my shoulder to get my full attention, and then continued in his calm but amusing voice. "I must now leave you to look for others to converse with on the beaches. Remember, no person ever realizes what they intend to do by adding 'maybe' into their speech. If you ever have anything to say, never use such a word, it implies a lack of knowledge.... Peace be your journey and self-discovery your learning!" Then the man walked away as quickly as he came.

I walked slowly the rest of that morning, examining the stillness of the day and admiring the openness of the man to come "randomly" to speak to me.

My thoughts were soon cast aside when I realized that the Israelis had approached my campsite.

"Neighbor? Hello?" the tallest of them was saying. He was standing almost directly in front of me. His name, I would find out, was Omer.

"Yes?" I responded, confused a bit by the perplexed expressions on their faces.

"We've been trying to get your attention for many minutes! You were zoned out in your mind!" one of them explained.

I laughed and assured them they had my full attention now. I invited them to join me on the patio of my mansion. We sat at the four chairs arranged around the old surfboard table. We looked past the twenty feet of grass onto the forty- or fifty-foot trees of the nature preserve. I was grateful that I had the best camp spot, as there were two small trees on both sides of my tent, blocking the walkway so that everyone could not stroll past and block the view of the preserve. Surely the area around my mansion was a far cry from the busy streets of tourists and backpackers in Byron Bay.

"This mansion is a little different than other ones I've seen!" said Daniel, a bearded, robust man about twenty-five years of age, with coffee-black hair and piercing maple eyes that complemented his raw, almond-colored skin. "Yes, the mansions we see in Israel are usually big and not made of polyester and nylon. But yours—yours is something else, my friend!"

I laughed and patted him on the shoulder auspiciously because I could already sense they were earnest-hearted men: a dying breed, I feared.

"Yes, this is simplicity. There is nowhere else I can dream of being," Omer pronounced, the oldest of the three, around twenty-seven, with a bob of curly raven hair that hung liberally around his chestnut face. He was the one who originally introduced himself. He said that they had driven up the coast for days in their camper van and were a little tired.

"Oh, come on, Omer, we don't get tired; time is an artificial construct yet to be proven. When we steer away from the limitations of linear time, electrifying energy is found," Daniel said, with the wit of a sage.

Then, Omer spoke intently. "You know, we have been traveling Australia for six months and have yet to meet an American willing to sit down and talk with us."

I told them I understood and said that all I wanted to do was listen to them unwind their minds. It would be an educational experience for me, I explained. Once I had expressed my desires, they spoke briefly in Hebrew. Then Omer turned back to me. He said that I was different from most people they'd met on this journey, and they'd been hoping to be able to meet and welcome someone like me into their circle of friendship.

"I guess it's the power of like minds attracting one another," I added knowingly.

There we sat, laughing in awe of our connection, and speaking of how wonderful it will be when the world as a whole can live in peace.

After a few weeks of hiking the beaches without a care in the world, I was sitting on my patio fingering through Dr. Bruce Lipton's book *Biology of Belief* when my friends approached: "We are heading to a huge musical festival, one of the largest in all of Australia…and we bought you a ticket. Would you care to join us?"

I readily accepted the invitation, not completely understanding their level of kindness. Later I discovered that they had paid $165 for my ticket. Their hearts were unique. They inspired me to serve others, whether it was with a smile or an offer to lunch.

The next sunrise, I zipped up my estate for the weekend to head up the east coast with them. We piled into their beige camper van that had space for eight people, though we only had four of us. There was a window sticker reading: No worries mate, life's all a game.

I sat in the backseat on a sofa-like seat bench while the three of them were in the front. It was an old van, with only two rows of seating, three seats per row, but the leather was comfortable and made for a smooth drive. I had plenty of legroom, despite the luggage and equipment.

While we continued up the coast along a lonely highway, I looked out the window at the surreal sea cliffs that jettisoned off the break of the unblemished shoreline. My eyes traveled upward toward the sky, above the distant green hills. Blue had always been my favorite color, but this particular shade—azure, I would call it—was a color so outstanding that I suspected it was a once-in-a-lifetime kind of sight. As we drove along a spectacular cliff, my eyes glued themselves onto the landscape. It was as if we were driving on the edge of the world.

I smiled with gratitude, resting my forehead against the window. As we continued, we kicked the occasional dish of small talk, mainly listening to Bob Marley's *Songs of Freedom* album from their iPod for the hour and a half drive to Griffith University, where the concert called "Good Vibrations" was. When I examined the situation, it was ironic: Griffith was the university I had planned to attend if I had stayed in college and traveled abroad. But life had other plans for me.

Upon arrival at the concert I threw on a straw hat to protect myself from the intense sun. The yellow fireball in the sky massaged my arms. As we bobbed and weaved through a sea of people, I smiled thinking of my white tank top decorated with Bob Marley's image. A large grassy area—about four football fields in length—was surrounded by enormous speakers and a dozen separate stages under huge white tents.

In the center where we found our place, all genres of music—from reggae to electronic—merged into one universal song of pleasure. I moved toward the reggae stage and stayed there for a very long time. Something about reggae has a way of syncing with my heart and easing my mind, carrying me into unfamiliar dimensions of creativity. Later, when I told a friendly African Rastafarian with dreadlocks how reggae makes me feel, he explained, "Dis' music make da' same beats per minute as da' average heart, mon'! About sixty!"

When Damian Marley, Bob Marley's son, came on stage, I let my soul feel the message of peace and individualism. Couples kissed one another, people danced, and hundreds smiled, entranced by the tranquilizing lyrics.

The concert contained a broad spectrum of ethnicities, which enlivened and fascinated me. I met people from all over—India, Canada, New Zealand, Africa, Asia, North and South America, as well as Europe. My friends and I moved to the rhythm for hours and concluded our day by listening to Cockatoo Paul. We left in the camper van to sleep at a rest stop on the side of the cliffs above the ocean.

That night I thought of Cockatoo Paul. He was as much of an individual as they come. He spoke to the crowd's heart, playing guitar, didgeridoo, and an eight-piece drum set, all while that cockatoo of his sat on his shoulder.

Cockatoo Paul had grown up on the streets. His parents left him behind, and he didn't want to live in foster homes, so he slept outside until he was twenty-two. He said that when he had no money he would sleep in front of a pizza parlor, where he'd eat the discarded food. But he wasn't asking for sympathy; he wanted us to know that *anything* and *everything* is possible. He'd made it to live his dream of performing weekly concerts, and he even owned his own business where he taught neglected Aborigines how to survive off the land.

I felt like he was speaking directly to me when he said that the only advice he had was to find something you enjoy doing and that you can become good at. Make that hobby your absolute obsession. Then make your obsession your profession, and you will never work a day in your life.

"We must understand that dreams are the language of life," he proclaimed to the crowd. He strummed an acoustic melody over his words: "Nobody is smarter than you. . . . This is your only life! When it ends, there's no reset button where you can go back and correct all the time you've wasted. . . . "Dream awake, don't live asleep, my brothers and sisters!"

Those final words were what kept me awake that night. I simply rested and watched the stars through the window as I dreamed of my dreams. I desired to maintain a state of awareness in my conscious mind, because it is what holds our present desires. I smiled in gratitude for my life until sunrise.

Find something you enjoy doing and that you can become good at. Make that hobby your absolute obsession. Then, make your obsession your profession and you will never work a day in your life.... We must understand that dreams are the language of life.

One Love

I see God in the man at the bus stop.
I see Allah in everyone who talks.
I see Jesus in the politicians.
I can feel the creator in the sun.
I talk to Buddha when I'm all alone.
I see Krishna atop his ruling throne.
Ra sings to me in the light of night stars.
Moses can part my mind's sea, near or far.
It's all the same, can't we just let it be?
We're all the same, one mind equally.
I see our source in the blue of your eyes
I know Jah force comes in all the sizes.
Black white brown green all races are divine.
So I'm gonna spread the love all through time.
We're all the same, can't we just let it be?
No worries, No worries,
It's in the water; it's in all the air.
The force of creation lives everywhere.
It's in the bombs we build I don't know why.
God's in the all impoverished children's cries
It's all the same; can't we just let it be?
One life to live free, no worries.

—Jake Ducey

One Small Visualization, One Giant Reward

Surfer's Paradise, February 20, 2011

> *A rock pile ceases to be a rock pile the moment a single man contemplates it, bearing within him the image of a cathedral.*
>
> —Antoine De Saint-Exupery

Our ride to the campground was silent. I sat in the back again. It would be the last time I would hang with my friends before they dropped me off and left town. With my eyes closed, I visualized meeting new kindred spirits. I smiled, knowing it would happen, because all of our desires are two things: the feeling that the desire exists or feeling the absence of it; sick or well, energized or tired, and rich or poor.

I reflected on the stagnation of tent life over the past three or so weeks. It was the same old routine without any new adventure—hiking, swimming in the ocean, using the computer in town, and sitting on my patio talking with friends. Asia was on my agenda, but where in Asia to go was still up in the air. After my friends dropped me off, I sat down for lunch at an old wooden picnic table near my tent. The picnic table resided beneath a tree that stretched her branches to shade its visitors from the pestering sun. I dug my bare feet into the sand and welcomed a spotless ladybug onto my finger. I knew it was a sign of good fortune. I placed it on the uneven wooden table and started eating.

Halfway through my meal of brown rice, broccoli, and carrots, a hulking physical specimen of a man, who resembled a giant-but-cuddly teddy bear, approached with a radiant-faced, blue-eyed girl at his side. At first glance I knew my call to the world had been answered. His name was Michael, from Germany, and hers was Joelle, from Canada.

While we made each other's acquaintances and talked about where we had been and where we were going, Joelle mentioned she'd just been approached on the beach by a butt-naked man who wanted her to swim with him. She laughed lightheartedly, then said seriously, "It just made me realize that I'm looking for more right now than simply tanning on the beach and wasting away.... There's an extended meditation program in Thailand that I'd really like to enter."

I patted the table in excitement, and I told her I'd be interested in meeting her there in the future. I cocked my head to the side with a smile. In response, her eyes lit up in the sunlight while Michael leaned forward to put his arm on my shoulder.

"This world never ceases to blow my mind," I told my new friends. "It seems that whenever I am ready for something, it manifests right before my eyes...like meeting the two of you.

I watched a few blackbirds await fallen food crumbs. I didn't know why they would want to eat food off the dirt. I watched them kiss, dance, and sing on a branch above us. Joelle's honey-colored hair shined while she said she'd be leaving the following night to head south to meet friends for a few weeks. Then she took my contact information.

When I finished eating, we walked to my tent. I felt God's right eye comfort me with its warm rays through the tree branches. I bit my lip in euphoria and rubbed my feet around on the fallen red and green leaves. Then I looked into Joelle's poetry-filled blue eyes while she spoke about meditation and how it had changed her life. I picked up a red leaf and traced my finger through its veins. A few lonely clouds passed.

Michael listened to us talk, and although he had never tried meditation, he thought it might help him break away from his past and into a better future. His voice grew solemn while he reflected on his past. The blue sky turned figuratively black.

I put my bare feet on the surfboard table. Unusually, the hot surface wax felt good because of the sun. We sat in a circle. The blue tarp covered most of the sun.

"My parents used to tell me to stay in my room all day," he said, taking a sip of water.

I thought about the paradox he seemed to be, his body so massive but his voice so innocent. "When I would ask why, they would tell me that they didn't have time for me because my birth wasn't expected…The words didn't bother me as much as my empty stomach did. Sometimes I would open the door to my room and walk out into the hallway to ask for supper, but no one would be home. I learned later in life that they would be partying into the early morning." He paused and our eyes locked onto him. "Unfortunately, there was no food in the house for me to eat, so I'd wait impatiently for them to feed me the next day. They did eventually, just never enough. I can remember my dad feeding me the remains of his milk from bowls of cereal," he stopped and asked us if he wanted to hear more. We nodded, and then he told us he had learned how to forgive them.

I gulped, but I had no saliva in my mouth. I was thankful life brought us together, because all the times I used to think I was somehow wronged were nothing compared to what he went through. My days believing life wasn't providing for me, my times in what I thought were awful moments of despair after my car accident, were really nothing compared to his story.

"I remember watching my parents feed the dog before me…. Usually, the dog even got more food. But imagination became a tool for me to pretend I was in a more accepting place. I dreamt that someday I would leave to travel the world, and I'd find all I ever needed."

He said that once he was able to work, he started to save money, and when he turned twenty-one, he had come to

Australia. He had been there for three years. "Whenever I was going through tough times, this other part of me would remind me that real dreamers don't quit, because it's how they communicate with the universe," he told us.

Michael's feet joined mine on the surfboard table. I wondered if his were dirtier. He closed his eyes for a few moments, and I suspected he was about to speak again. After a minute, he looked at Joelle and me and said, "Happy are those who hold beautiful visions, because one day they'll realize them!"

Joelle and I looked at him intently, smiling, but saying nothing. It was quiet for a while and then the crickets broke the silence. The sun was playing musical chairs with the moon. I turned on a green electric lantern and placed it on the surfboard. My friends and I spoke softly for a brief time more about life and love and beauty. Then Joelle and Michael said their good-byes. If it were meant to be, I'd see them again.

Happy are those who hold beautiful visions,
because one day they'll realize them!

Hitchhike to the Heart

Gold Coast, February 23, 2011

Only those who will risk going too far can possibly find out how far one can go.

—T. S. Elliot

My shoulder-high tent was wearing on me, and I was ready to live with a renewed purpose. But this Western world's comfort zone was difficult to give up, and so I spent the next nights at the campground, mingling with sociable strangers from all over the world. I observed the swirls of people and their drunken dilemmas of losing their traveling partners, then watching them magically reappear, stumbling and slurring moments later. I listened as they made plans to go into town, before losing each other, searching for one another, and then finding each other a few feet away.

One night, during a relentless storm, I hid beneath a chest-high palm tree that extended its arms in shelter like a patio overhang. Hours could've passed before my shadow and I trudged the muddy confines of the campgrounds to my one-time palace. I walked slowly, feeling the ground with my feet so as not to slip. The edges of my toes touched first, then my heels. I placed my left foot down, slipped forward, stumbling over something. That something, I was soon to know, was a drunken couple making "love" in the pitfalls of a miniswamp. I hit the ground and splatted into water and mud. One thing led to another. Then I found myself entangled in their baby-making process as my feet flipped over theirs. Their naked bodies expressed repulsion while they caressed the twigs and dirt. I sprung up quickly like a wild animal roused from sleep.

I contemplated my fall when I got back to my tent. The area was normally a sort of walkway, but due to the unforgiving storm, the geography had been morphed. I brushed away remnants of the encounter.

Being that it was three in the morning, I was thankful to know there was a Greyhound bus at five to Coolangatta, the town where I had originally begun my Australian journey. Sleep was the last thing on my mind. Moving on was the first. We hardly ever realize that we can cut anything out of our lives, at any time, in the blink of an eye. Thus, I threw my objects of self into my backpack at a record pace.

All packed with the exception of the water-logged pillow, I thanked my mansion tent for all its unforgettable memories, and, like magic, the rain lessened as if earth's spirit, Gaia, was directing me to leave this land. I waved good-bye to my tent, simply leaving it be. While I hiked through the muddy campgrounds on my way out, I made sure to steer clear of the couple I'd intruded on. Meanwhile, the sparkling odor of eucalyptus and the hypnotic scents of tea tree, golden wattles, and evergreens all sent their condolences for my departure.

Nearing the exit of the campgrounds, I came to a blonde woman who was manicuring her toenails with twigs under the main patio light. She spoke quickly, stridently, and loudly, as if she believed that through vocal thrust alone she could make people listen. But they weren't.

"We have a tent quitter!" she exclaimed to a nonexistent audience, pausing only to ingest imaginary laughter from the illusory crowd before going on.

Drawing on my fine command of the English language, I said nothing.

"You aren't cut out for this kind of life, kid. Go on and find whatever it is you are looking for while we stay right here." Her voice was bitter, as if I was rejecting her lifestyle by leaving so abruptly.

That was just it. I had begun to feel as if I were "staying right there," rather than evolving and learning more about this mysterious world and myself.

I laughed at her remark and said kindly, "Thank you and I hope you find what you search for as well." I continued on toward the bus station.

When I arrived in town it appeared I was the only person awake. I wandered in circles, half asleep, balancing on the curb, killing the few hours until the five o'clock bus swept me up. I drummed my fingernails on the stop sign.

The rain had subsided completely. I could feel the stillness of the moment while I looked at the empty shops across the street. The somber haze from the night's storm was beginning to lose its grip over the full moon. I watched an early-rising snail slug its way across the cement. It must have been pleased, for it didn't have to battle with the heat that habitually blazed the walkway like a frying pan.

The area was as still as death until the morning freight train blared suddenly: *Boom! Boom! Boom!*

The colossal steel log of transportation barked, and then it was stiller than ever. I saw no Greyhound, no cars at all, and thirst was talking at full volume to my tongue. I moved under a knotted tree and not twenty eye blinks passed before a silver BMW of deceptive beauty broke the simmering hush of late dawn.

"How-de-do, stranger?" a man in his midthirties said, poking his head out the window. "What are you looking for this time of the day? Don't you know the Greyhound doesn't run early on Mondays?"

I had no clue it was Monday. *If time flies, why wear a watch at all,* I thought. Then I told him I was trying to head north a few hours to Coolangatta, where I had begun my travels.

The man introduced himself as Mark and offered me his hand from the driver's side of the car.

I had learned as a youth that you can tell a lot about a man by his handshake, and Mark's steady grip spoke volumes. "How about I give you a lift?" he offered.

I paused for a moment, inspecting him and his bronzed olive skin, which fit tightly to his cheeks and made his dimples shine kindly. His chocolate-colored eyes were full of hope and success.

"No need to be in fear," he added with an inviting Australian voice, the kind of vocals that the ears can't help but enjoy.

A phrase began to beat in my mind with a sort of intoxicating excitement: *You'll never know anything if you don't try.*

He seemed harmless, and because I had been visualizing meeting people who would guide me on my journey, I trusted that the universe had led him to me. Besides, I needed a ride, and he was offering one for free.

I walked to the passenger door, flung it open, and plopped myself next to him. This journey was not about playing it safe, I reminded myself. It was about taking chances, risks, and interesting, long-shot weirdo bets, making ourselves vulnerable to show the world that we have no fear of realizing our dreams; and once we do go beyond our fear, it provides for us. This being true, I had no reason not to hitch a ride with a complete stranger that I'd known for some thirty seconds.

"Some water?" he asked, handing me an unopened and chilled liter while we rode away in a flurry of dust that surely displeased the snail I'd seen.

I swallowed swigs greedily, gulping mightily, before remembering what I had read about how a man's character is exemplified also in how he eats and drinks. I put the cap back on and thanked him.

I examined his modest clothes: a white crewneck with ocean-blue jeans. My hair sailed back with the breeze that swept in through the open window, while I listened to his voice tell me what occupied his accomplished life: He was married (he wore a whopping, gold wedding ring), had two children (a boy and girl), and owned a chain of successful organic food stores. He also told me that he had no formal education, no college degree.

"You can live for many causes, but can only die for one.... When you know what that one is then you must be brave enough to say good-bye to your old life so that you may welcome the new," he said in a voice that sounded eerily like the late Steve Erwin, crocodile hunter.

I nodded and he continued speaking, "When the dreamer finally controls the dream, the dream can become the masterpiece it was always been meant to be."

Out of the womb of my seemingly purposeless travels, the wind had blown me toward this synchronistic opportunity to learn from this man. "What's your advice to someone who is trying to live their dreams?" I asked.

He placed his index finger over his lips in contemplation while the muscles in his commanding arm shifted. "I'll say this first," he said. "Nearly the entire world believes they are incapable of accomplishing great things, so they set mediocre standards for themselves." He paused for a moment to emphasize his last sentence. "If you have a high standard, it's easy to hit grand slams while the rest of the people are looking for occasional wild pitches to move them around the bases."

I listened intently to everything he said, soaking it in and silently thanking life for this opportunity as well as for the unbelievably blue sky. He told me that if there's no one pursuing what you're after, that's even better, because originality becomes greatness. He advised me to do one thing: write down definite life intentions, because paper has a better memory than the mind.

"Once we know our life vision," he said, "then it's a matter of commitment, because when we give up, we are really giving up on ourselves."

I was filled with gratitude for this impromptu lesson, and I thanked him for sharing his knowledge with me. I stuck my head out of the window and into the wind. The small green hills on the side of the road made for an energizing sight.

He smiled. "I guess this is a little more of a memorable ride than the Greyhound ride, huh, buddy?"

I nodded in agreement.

There was silence for a few moments.

"Well, in life you ultimately have two choices: to choose things that inspire you, or things that expire you. Decide now what's best for you!"

I knew I had chosen an inspiring action by hitching a ride with him. Even still, I had no idea how much time had passed and was surprised to see that I recognized we were in Coolangatta. "Man!" I said with disappointment. "Looks like I'm almost at my stop."

Before I hopped out of the car in front of the hostel, where I'd be spending the night, I thanked Mark for sharing his wisdom.

"No worries, mate," he replied. "Remember that whether you're a million in one or one of millions is up to you."

I smiled in understanding and agreement. When I closed the car door and grabbed my backpack, I felt a newfound confidence in me: I deserved to set high standards for what I wanted from life. I knew nothing deserved abundance and love more than my own heart. I grinned widely as I walked up the familiar concrete steps.

In life, you ultimately have two choices:
to choose things that inspire you,
or things that expire you.
Decide now what's best for you!

Friendship Beyond Words

Gold Coast, February 24, 2011

> *A friend, one in which I may speak my thoughts aloud in front of, may well be reckoned the masterpiece of nature.*
>
> —Ralph Waldo Emerson

Human activities such as sleeping hadn't crossed my mind in more than forty-eight hours. A thin ray of moonlight creeping through the cracks of the curtains in the ten-person hostel room told me it was well after eleven o'clock. I had been on the beach morning to night for the last two days since Mark had dropped me off. I was so inspired after meeting with him that I set a goal to write at least five poems per day in my journal, as well as jot down everything I could remember about our conversation.

I had been up all night, the last days surpassing my goal, and I felt alive, very alive, though I had slept little to none. While I rested in my bed, I looked around to see eight of my nine roommates asleep. I said my thanks to life for such a quiet room, although I briefly wondered as to the whereabouts of the last roommate.

While I lay there I was reminded of something Fernando had said: "The body can thrive off only four hours of sleep. Mothers do it all the time with newborn children. If you are going to get what you desire in life, you have to change your relationship with your pillow and sheets."

I knew Fernando was right and tried my best not to complain to myself about my lack of sleep.

Bam! Bam!

The door to the room catapulted open. I could see the silhouette of a man holding a bottle of something I assumed to be alcohol. He flicked the lights, once, twice, five times. Then he plopped onto the bed adjacent to mine. He left the lights on. I could practically see his eyeballs roll out of his head in utter intoxication.

He smelled of something awful. I could tell pretty much without looking that he hadn't showered in days, if not weeks. I didn't understand why because the showers were free at the hostel. His face radiated an age somewhere around forty or fifty, but it was tough to tell whether he wore wrinkles or not because he was so dirty. I smiled, realizing immediately it was a test from life to see if I could keep my momentum going amidst such a disturbance. I knew there would always be tests, and I took this one on with a big grin.

"Are you alright?" I asked, before deciding I'd say no more to him.

"I wassa…I wassa…" he supplied another imaginary verb with the wave of his finger, before breaking into a sickening cough. The *harawwrr!* sounded like it had come from a very angry bear.

When his howls reached a crescendo, I jumped out of bed, grabbed all my belongings, and exited the room. I left the madness behind for the other roommates to figure out as soon as I realized it wasn't going to stop anytime in the near future.

I opened the door, stepping into the dark hostel hallway and nearly toppled down a flight of stairs. When I regained balance, I saw a man in his late twenties smiling at me enchantingly as he leaned against the wall. He welcomed me into his room with a hand gesture. He had clearly heard the ruckus coming from my room and had come out to see how he could be of assistance. Seeing me, he knew. His midnight-black hair was sparingly streaked with slivers of nimble brightness. His smile was a human portrait of everlasting hope that I hadn't been blessed to see since leaving Fernando, and before that, my mother.

In particularly broken English he told me his name was Tetsu and that he was from Japan. He had the room to himself and wanted to share it with me because of the undesirable circumstances in the next room. His words were cut off by another yelp from the drunken man a few doors down. He smiled, depicting eternal understanding, although I realized he actually didn't understand what I was saying in the slightest.

"I sorry know only ten percent of what you say in English. Me English very poor," he laughed.

Our ears couldn't understand one another past the basics. There was a language barrier more profound than the Great Wall of China. Ironically, I sensed an immediate mutual understanding beyond words. For a moment, in between my breaths, I could see situations I experienced in Guatemala where I'd communicated with the children without the use of sound. I knew the universal language was beyond human noises, that the heart speaks no words, only vibrations.

We made eye contact, and I could see an agreement in his eyes that we would come to know one another on a clairvoyant level. The clock was ticking to a late hour. Although we didn't get far chatting, I'd intuitively understood much of his soul, because our bursts of laughter from not understanding one another had me believe that we would become close friends, though we could not speak too much.

Minutes later, I fell blissfully into the dominion of dreams for the first time in many days.

I sprung into consciousness in the morning. I'd had a vivid dream that I was in Indonesia, where I met a local healer. Dreams didn't usually stay with me upon awakening at the hostels since my sleep wasn't all that sound. However, this morning, having slept well, I did remember my dream and I knew it was a definite sign to follow my instinct and make that my next stop.

Before a breakfast of eggs, I searched the computer at the lab next door for the week's flights to Bali. Through synchronicity, I found one the following day out of the local Gold Coast airport. I was set to fly early in the morning and would be leaving the hostel before sunrise. I had a heart filled with warmth, for it was abnormal to find such a sensational deal on such short notice. I knew I was heading toward memories that would remain with me forever.

When Tetsu awoke, we decided to go on a full-day hike together, which came about by me asking him, "Walk? Walk? Walk?" until he understood.

Despite our inability to converse, I felt very comfortable around my new friend. It was as if our souls were communicating and getting to know each another, like we were sharing things telepathically. We walked easily along a glittering green and ageless hillside, running parallel to the blue horizon. The ocean guided the sun's reflection off it like a mirror reflecting light.

Unknown to our everyday problem-solving minds, Tetsu and I were walking the path to a village of eternal friendship, where language wasn't necessary. It was a realm where presence alone became the presents of companionship. We carried on the day with jovial bursts of laughter at our failed attempts to communicate traditionally.

As I studied Tetsu, I sensed a genuine aura of peace and fulfillment emanating from him. I detected a sophisticated level of simplicity that he taught through his demeanor and body language, like a true master. No jingles of jargon from vocalized examples were necessary.

The hours passed and the sun began to plummet lazily. We were nearing the end of a time that I was sure neither of us would ever forget. I led the way to the last of the single-lane paths that reconnected by the beach near our hostel.

"Your pants, no good!" he said in fragmented English.

I looked at him with a brow that illustrated my lack of understanding. *Did he not like my pants?*

I watched as he laughed and wiped the dirt off a twig and snapped it in half, continuing to point at his buttocks.

"Oh gosh!" I said, after looking at the back of my jeans.

I had a rip in them larger than the hole in the Australian ozone layer, where my bare skin peeked through.

"You do on purpose?" he questioned innocently with a wholehearted grin.

I shook my head no; I hadn't the faintest clue they were tattered.

"American fashion?" Tetsu asked, collapsing in hysterics as if he'd been hit by a boulder.

I also broke out into laughter thinking of the eighty or so people we had passed throughout the day who must have noticed my fashion gash.

As we continued back into town, it became impossible to make eye contact without chuckling out of control. I stopped to catch my breath and realized I was receiving a strenuous abdominal workout from the beaming smiles and laughter.

My foot rested on an Indian-red rock. The last of the sun sat on the horizon like a delicate lotus atop still water. My mind reset into stillness at the rosy red and golden bubbled clouds, which filled with the remains of the sun's rays. I wanted to get inside the majestic billows and float away toward my dreams. Tetsu jiggled in agreement like a bobble-head doll. We shared our mutual feelings easily on an emotional level, as we watched the life-giving fireball in the sky seemingly morph into the secretive cool oval.

On the horizon, glimpses of distant ships lit the vista of the world with their cherry-blinking bows, while the stars began jazzing overhead. I wanted to hoist up an Aboriginal crossbow and shoot them down to collect and harness their power. Then I remembered I didn't need their power because I was already unlimited and full of potential.

That evening, after we had showered and put on fresh clothes, Tetsu and I sat down to share dinner. I watched with amusement as he nearly choked on his food every time the tear in my jeans flashed into his head. "Your clothes broken," he said, to explain why the food was making him gag.

"You are a good friend," I told him. "One of a kind!"

"I get great feeling," he said, closing his eyes in search for more words to describe our connection, but could not.

I understood.

After I stuffed my bags, we sat in our adjacent beds, struggling once more to converse before sleep.

"You girlfriend in America?" he questioned.

I shook my head no. I explained as well as I could that I had yet to find a girl in America who had a heart and mind I could relate to.

Silence filled the empty space.

"All girls in America eat McDonalds?" he asked with a confused whisper.

Puzzled, I silently indicated that I didn't understand the question. Then, waiting and smiling with great anticipation, I watched him search through a portable dictionary for the words to explain. After a few minutes, he found what he was looking for. Then he fell off his bed onto the floor like a cat who'd become dizzy chasing its own tail. Once he caught his breath, he said, "I think you say you have no girlfriend because girls in America eat fast food!"

I felt the bubbling laughter rising from my stomach. I'd laughed so much with my new friend that I had to stand up and throw my hands above my head so I wouldn't vomit from all the laugher. (It had happened twice in my life.)

Tetsu kicked his feet in the air like a dog, and seemingly hours later he said, "Never have I laughed more." Then he paused and looked through his dictionary before continuing, "I will miss you, friend."

I smiled with gratitude and told him the same. As we returned to our beds, I tried to quiz him about life in the rice fields and countryside but realized in no time that my questions were merely proposed to the looming and ripened moon. He didn't understand a word. We sat in comfortable silence through the remainder of the night, though our hearts intermingled loudly.

I knew the universal language was beyond human noises, that the heart speaks no words, only vibrations.

Part Four

Indonesia: Worrying Limits Possibilities

Trusting Life Through Uncertainty

Gold Coast Airport, March 1, 2011

> *Do not go where the path may lead, go instead where there is no path and leave a trail.*
>
> —Ralph Waldo Emerson

I eagerly awoke to a good morning song from my 4:00 am alarm. I hoisted the bundle of my belongings atop my back and stepped into the warm Australian morning air. While I waited for the bus that would take me to the airport, I examined the place I was leaving behind. It was a beautiful one that would always hold a space in my heart. The song of silence playing in the air was unusual for the small city, and so I carefully considered its meaning. It led me to humorously conclude that there was no busyness because the whole city was silently watching me depart, thanking me for spending time there.

The ordinary busyness of city life made its first appearance of the day when a young, attractive woman lunged for the first taxi that pulled up. I processed her rush and smirked with relief that I was not in a similar predicament. I had no need to hurry, at least not yet. As I was thinking about my good fortune, the screeching of the bus brakes put a stop to my self-reflection. I eagerly climbed aboard.

Just as I arrived at the airline desk, a clerk on her way to her morning break told me that the flight would likely be delayed until the following day because there were mechanical problems, making the plane unusable. If it were to fly that day, the size of the plane would have to be downgraded because there were no more available planes of the originally scheduled size; only half the passengers would be able to board. Meanwhile, the rest of the passengers would have to wait until the following day, but would receive a free flight to anywhere in Australia. Additionally, the flight would definitely be postponed at least seven hours for the mechanical reasons.

Although Australia had been a fine home for the past seven weeks, I had no desire to stay longer. Thus, I told myself that I *would* get on that flight *today*. I was the first to pitch camp at the airline check-in. Three hours passed, but still no other employees arrived. Some hours later, one counter opened. Positivity flowed through the crevices of my brain as I hopped up. *I will get on this flight,* I repeated to myself.

"Next in line," the attendant called out.

I walked to the counter with confidence and what I was certain was a permanent smile.

"Can I have your first and last name, please," the employee asked.

"Are you crazy? If I give them to you, what's my name going to be then?" I joked.

She kind of smiled, and I don't know if she understood. She looked at me and asked for my bank card and identification. While I looked, I checked off *never make jokes at airports again* from my list.

I reached into my pocket and came out with a few receipts. I smashed my hand into my other pockets. Nothing. Pausing to take deep breaths, I examined the rest of my belongings. My wallet wasn't there either. *No worries, it had to be in my backpack.* I raced through every compartment. No wallet.

"Excuse me, ma'am, I think I may have lost my wallet waiting in line. I only have a passport right now. Please, could you book me for the flight check-in, and I'll come back shortly."

She nodded with an empathetic smile. I picked my passport up from the counter and set off running through the terminal. While I did this I began to learn that the difference between running and walking is a lot more apparent when you've lost all your belongings. My wallet was nowhere to be found. I laughed, half helplessly, amused by my predicament. No one could help me. Ironically, I was in a place brimming with people, but I was all alone. I ran through the airport like a bloodhound following a fresh scent.

When I knew I would not find my wallet, I concluded that life was playing a joke on me—testing me the way I had been testing it. I considered my situation and options carefully: All I had left was my passport and some Australian money. Either I could remain in Australia until I got a replacement bank card, or I could test my fortune and head off to Indonesia with a pocket full of money and positive thinking.

While I thought, I reminded myself of the principle of calculated risks: take a chance and step into the unknown with faith, and the universe will balance your experience. After all, there's no reason not to take risks—life is brief in the eye of eternity.

Back in line I told the woman at the counter my situation. She checked me in with my passport, and then informed me that it is mandatory when entering Indonesia to have a return ticket. Although she didn't need to see my credit card, she said she could not let me board the plane without an exit ticket from the country.

I looked at her sorry face, seeing that she wished for me to get on the flight. Regardless, my heart stopped, but laughter kick-started it back up like a motorcycle's reserve gas tank. I had no money for another ticket. Not only that, it was against my way of traveling to have a set return date. I wished to wander in absolute freedom.

I told her I had just less than a hundred Australian dollars and begged for her to book me the cheapest return flight humanly possible, with plans to change it when I was ready to leave. That way I would have a bit of cash left after paying for the cheap Indonesian visa. And that moment I also came to a realization: I could always double my money by folding it in half and putting it back in my pocket.

The levels of my patience, maturity, and sense of humor were being put to the test. The hard part for me wasn't recognizing the challenge but getting through it. Anybody who has been in unusual circumstances knows that without the ability to smile and laugh at the situation, we'd go *completely* insane.

I saw sympathy for my plight in the attendant's eyes, and I could tell she was going to give me a deal that wasn't normally available. She booked me a sixty-dollar flight out of Indonesia to Malaysia, a month after my landing. I think she was as shocked as I was at the price she'd found in her computer system. I was saved, at least partially. I still had no wallet, just a passport and about nineteen dollars after paying for my visa. Nonetheless, I had an iPod and a camera that I figured could be exchanged for cash if I became desperate for money.

Excitement coursed through my veins. Ever since I was a child I'd been told that if I played with fire I would get burned. But I had also been told that we shouldn't believe everything we hear. Instead, I was relying on my own abilities to trust. While I looked around the crowded airport, I knew that if I breathed and believed, eventually I'd expand my capacity to handle the new and unfamiliar. Putting my backpack on, I told myself that when we step outside of our comfort zones, it may seem scary at first. But the truth is that it's often the mind that tells us of the dangers. While I walked toward security, I was aware that the *real* danger was when I believed in the limits of the mind.

Problems like this activate the lessons we've learned from our parents and others when we were children. In my case, my parents had taught me well, and so I knew that if I put forth all my positivity and communication skills I would be all right. I affirmed to life that I wasn't scared and peered beyond the negativity. With each step forward, I gave my appreciation for being able to get on a flight that over a hundred people missed because of the downgraded size of the plane. I was using gratitude as a means to consciously create beautiful future experiences. I had read and learned firsthand that gratitude naturally raises our energy level to the highest vibration possible, and this allows the universe to provide abundance for us.

I said good-bye to the chance of recovering my lost wallet as I passed through security. The guard raised his eyebrows and shook his head when I told him I was going to Indonesia without my wallet. He clearly thought I was crazy. And although I was exhausted and needed to rest as soon as possible, I opted to decline the TSA's X-ray scanner. Not wanting to be shot with cancer-causing rays, it had become my custom to request a physical search.

The TSA agent rummaged through my backpack as if I had just been caught smuggling opium. I smiled while she inspected my harmonica as if I had hidden drugs Johnny Cash–style within the small instrument. Apparently, if you have long hair and decline to be scanned, you are guilty until proven innocent. All was fine with me, and anyway, I welcomed the entertainment. And at last, I was let go.

I eagerly approached the gate, only to discover that the flight had been delayed yet another hour. Impatience played upon the faces of my fellow travelers. The delay wasn't ideal for me either, considering the plane would land after midnight, and I had nowhere to stay and didn't know anyone. I embraced faith, believing lady luck would kiss me with relief. I reminded myself that everything works out when we cease to worry. I closed my eyes and visualized everything unfolding magically.

When I climbed aboard, I was thankful for an exit-row seat. I drifted off to sleep before the 747 metal bird left the ground. I had been up for around twenty hours. Plus, losing my wallet had wiped me out. I could feel my nose dripping. When I closed my eyes, I assured myself that I was not getting sick...then I assured myself some five hundred times more. Because there is also a *no-cebo effect,* which is the opposite of the *placebo effect,* meaning that too many negative thoughts about some "illness" can get you very sick…even kill you.

But before I fell asleep, I thought about what cell biologist Dr. Bruce Lipton had said in one of his books: our cells as a whole *are in awareness of the physical environment through physical sensations.* And not by coincidence, that's the same dictionary definition of perception! Thus, I was aware that our own *perception* controls cellular and biological behavior.

While I nodded into deep sleep, my soul said everything would be all right. I knew this would be one of the bedtime stories I'd someday tell my grandkids.

We touched ground sometime after midnight. I filled out the immigration card with a fake hotel address because I didn't know where to stay. I knew nothing about Indonesia, except that it was near the ocean. Once I exited the plane, two local men grabbed my things and carried them to the front. *Great. What a lovely place. They even carry your bags for you. Yes, everything will be fine!* I thought.

We walked to the front of the airport where they set my bags down. The man stuck out his hand for money. I didn't see it coming.

"I'm sorry, my friend, but I only have nineteen dollars," I said.

His face expressed no amusement or sympathy. I forked over five dollars, but he insisted on two more. In the unfamiliar darkness, I walked to a hotel-accommodation center nearby that a doorman pointed me to. Two young women were working at the counter and spoke fluent English. I flirted with them. Unfortunately, it was too late and almost all of the rooms were snagged, but I got one with breakfast for eight dollars. That left me with four dollars. While waiting for my free taxi ride to the room, one of the women who had clearly been interested in me, as evidenced by her lustful grin, came from behind the counter with a grocery bag stuffed with bottles of water and bread.

"For you," she said with a mix of humor and amazement at my having arrived in her country without money.

I was blown back by her kindness. I said nothing and gave her a massive hug instead. Her friend watched from a close distance and smiled. The women exchanged some words in Indonesian and then laughed. I figured they were questioning my sanity, and I laughed too. It wasn't the first time my sanity had been questioned, and I was okay with it.

When the taxi arrived, I thanked the women and hugged them in public this time, rather than in the accommodation room. It caught them off guard. It made me think that white tourists usually don't hug locals, especially women. Not that it is outlawed, just uncommon. Regardless, they laughed, seeming fine with the situation.

From the moment the gas-eating, cyclical-transport vehicle began feasting on fossil fuels, I knew my driver spoke little English.

"Do you like Bob Marley?" I asked with a smile. This question had broken the ice on many occasions in Guatemala.

Smiling back, he threw his arms in the air to signal a lack of understanding. Laughing, I attempted to explain to him my situation. With little money I couldn't pay him a tip for the drive. Somewhere in the language barrier my words were lost.

"Women? You want local woman for your hotel room?"

"No, no, no! I am sorry; that isn't what I said. Please, I don't want that!" I laughed, bordering on hysterics and praying he understood me. I hoped my next stop wouldn't be a prostitute den.

We were silent the rest of the ride. He had no idea what I was saying. Moments later, Bob Marley came on the radio. I sang. He didn't. I tried to tell him that the musician I was asking about earlier was on the radio, but again he didn't understand. I laughed.

Since we could not talk, the ride was relatively silent besides the music. I looked out the window into the dark street, seeing small white shops, but not many people at all. Just motorcycles, lots of motorcycles. We arrived at the hotel around 3:00 am, after a short five-minute drive. Immediately after I checked in, I went straight to bed. I didn't even bother to turn on the dim light.

As I drifted off to sleep, I contemplated my situation. I was pretty sure the next day was Friday. I figured the banks would be closed for the weekend and wouldn't reopen until Monday. I had few options: I could call my mom, which would cost me all the cash I had left. She could wire me some money, which still wouldn't arrive until Monday, or…I could prostitute myself out for the pleasure of the Indonesian women. The latter seemed both inconceivable and unnecessary, but it sure made me laugh, and I needed a good smile. I chose neither option, deciding to see what the universe had planned for me. And with that, I fell into an easy sleep.

I reminded myself of the principle of calculated risks; take a chance and step into the unknown with faith, and the universe will balance your experience.

Saved by Faith

Kuta Square, March 2, 2011

> *You better take care of me Lord, if you don't you're gonna have me on your hands.*
>
> —Hunter S. Thompson

I awoke five hours later to the musty smell of mildew and realized that I'd been overcharged for the room. I rinsed my body in the small cold shower and headed down for breakfast. More bread. While eating, I met an Indonesian man around my age from another island on vacation with his girlfriend. They both spoke good English, and so we got to talking. Like the others I'd encountered, they thought my situation was comical, but I could also tell that my bravery had earned their respect. It was helpful to be able to make people laugh, but being admired by them was also helpful because it seemed to make them want to assist me. They offered me a ride into town believing it would be my best shot at finding help. As I gathered my belongings, they offered me a cigarette. I declined and told them that smoking kills. And if you're killed, you've lost a very important part of your life.

When we got in their car they affirmed that I had been ripped off for my room. Only a few minutes later they dropped me off in Kuta Square, the main center in the city of Kuta, Bali. Sweat stuck to my body while my gear pressed on my back. Perspiration was burning my eyes. I hadn't dared take more than a few steps before I was approached by some local men who were trying to sell me anything they had.

"Dude, I have no money. I lost my wallet. I'm sorry," I told them, but they didn't seem to believe me.

One of the men put his arm around me and guided me toward their sitting area near a light post. He was around forty years old, and only half my size, with a raven-colored mustache, short matching hair, a clever smile, and pure eyes. He introduced himself as Rudy. In turn, I shared my name.

"What are you looking for?" he asked.

I didn't know. I was chasing life, love, and laughter.

"I don't really know," I explained. "I lost my wallet before I boarded the plane, and I have almost no money left."

At first, hysterical laughter was the only response. Then, regaining his composure, Rudy asked, "Why on earth would you come here if you lost your wallet? Don't you know the banks are closed for three days?"

I shook my head. Then one of the other men asked me what I had of monetary value. I told them about my camera and iPod.

"Listen here, Jake. You are a good guy, I can tell," Rudy said, putting his arm on my shoulder and standing with ease. "You aren't like other tourists. I know this because no one would come here without money. I will take care of you until your mother can get you cash. You need food, you tell me. You need transport or hospitality, you tell me. You need phone, or anything, please let me know. We are all family here, you know?"

When I gazed into Rudy's eyes, I could see he wasn't looking for anything except to help. I was sure he was my first gift from the wind of chance in this new land. After a few minutes of smiles, I hopped on the back of his motorcycle and he took me to his friend's hotel. Negotiating with the owner, Rudy not only got a cheaper price than listed, but also worked out a deal so that I wouldn't have to pay until I had more money.

My body shouted its thanks as I unloaded my bags from my shoulders to give myself a rest from the scorching heat and dripping humidity. I didn't know how the locals worked on the streets all day in that weather. It was like a sauna, and they were beyond human.

After I had settled into my new nest, I sprang back onto Rudy's motorcycle out in the city square. He introduced me to the rest of his friends, who, as I suspected they would, laughed at my predicament. It was a mass of wild hilarity while they discussed my odyssey and asked me questions. Then, without even asking if I was hungry, which I was, Rudy handed me a wax-paper bag full of local food: *nasi* (rice), *telur* (eggs), and *sambal* (chile). We ate on the curb in the center of Kuta Square.

Countless shops selling everything no one really needed laced the sidewalk, boxing us inside with walls of concrete. While we ate, I watched as hundreds of motorcycles circled the roundabout on their way through the town, while tourists wandered the side of the road, dodging the speeding cyclists from time to time. I'd never sat smack in the middle of a motorcycle competition for obvious reasons, but now I was getting a firsthand experience of what it would be like.

Besides the compassion and friendliness of the locals, I also noticed that none of the tourists seemed to be interested in interacting with them. With hands full of shopping bags, they moved along with blank faces, staring disapprovingly whenever they caught a glimpse of me sitting on the dirty ground with the locals. I smiled at them. The truth was that life had become immeasurably more joyful since I stopped taking it seriously.

After lunch, Rudy escorted me to the phone-service store. There, he proceeded to buy me a phone and a SIM card. I was awed by his kindness and hugged him. He laughed at me.

"You are my friend, Jake. I know you would do the same for me if I had no money in your country."

A part of me thought that I'd do the same, and I hoped I would, but I couldn't compare my generosity to his, for it far exceeded my own.

I put my arm on his shoulder and said thank you in a soft and sincere voice. He looked at me and told me to stop saying thanks because they see it as an obligation to give without expecting a return of any sorts.

Next, Rudy invited me to his house. I hadn't a clue what to expect, but I knew it would be much different from mine in San Diego. I bounced onto the back of his motorcycle once again. As we made our way toward the residential district, I took note of the poverty-stricken area. The homes were even smaller than those in Guatemala but were still made of concrete. Like the setups I'd seen before, the porch was usually a shop or restaurant, and the back was where the families lived. Many had hung their clothes to dry on a line facing the street. I smiled at the locals sitting on the curbs in front of their shops as we road by; most smiled back.

Rudy laid the engine to rest in an area free of tourists. I felt no fear. I instinctively knew from the moment I'd met him that I was in safe hands. We walked through an alley where the Balinese locals either smiled or stared at me. It was a development of concrete shacks stacked on top of each other and beside one another, separated by old blankets. Dirt alleys divided the "apartments," where children played games until they saw me. Once they did, they began to chase us. I must've received thirty hugs and high-fives. One lady even stopped us to take a picture of me with the children on her phone. They were as amused and excited as I was. Minus losing my wallet, it was exactly what I had pictured when arriving in Indonesia. I was as close as anyone could ever come to their culture. I guess sometimes we have to give up the good to get the great, even though it may feel like a sacrifice at the time.

We approached Rudy's home. His wife, their three children, and two of their friends greeted me outside. They spoke little English. We all laughed because we couldn't communicate the way Rudy and I could. We stepped toward their home. No doors. No windows. No air conditioning. No Western luxuries. He pulled the blanket off the front, and we entered. Gray concrete everywhere—with beautiful Balinese art hanging in every which way to decorate the eight-by-eight-foot room. We sat down crisscross on the recently swept floor. After introducing me to his wife, friends, and children, Rudy said, "More food."

I wasn't hungry, but I knew it would be disrespectful to refuse. I was also aware that I didn't exactly have enough money to buy my own meals later, so I took advantage of the offering. I didn't know what the plate had on it, but I ate it anyway. Midway through the meal, I finally asked what it was.

Rudy looked up and smiled. "Coconut-fried cow and fish. Fresh you see. It still has the eyes."

I had been a vegetarian for eighteen months before I got to Bali. I didn't think coconut cow and fish with eyes on it were categorized as vegetables. I didn't care. It was a once in a lifetime opportunity. As I continued eating, I heard much laughter and conversation in Balinese. Rudy told me that his family and neighbors, who watched us from outside the door, thought I was very interesting; no other tourists would eat their food.

"White people always eat at McDonalds," he snickered.

I laughed too, as I took another bite of the alien lunch. I felt like an extraterrestrial, but at least I was on a planet where the locals were respectful, generous, and interested in me.

"Where do you sleep?" I asked, looking around the room.

"Where you are sitting now, my whole family does," he explained.

I swallowed my tongue. Love was the only thing by which they measured life. It was obvious from the looks of it that they spent their entire day making one another laugh, then bundling up to sleep just inches from one another. I looked at the concrete floor in disbelief.

A little while later we set off to the city. On our way out of Rudy's house, I was "attacked" by friendly children who were like a pride of lions preying on a wounded deer. They grabbed at my limbs and hugged me, and then proceeded to run away, only to return to hug me again. I couldn't stop laughing. Neither could the children or Rudy. The love and goodwill intoxicated me.

When we were back at the square, Rudy's friends asked me why I didn't want to do the usual tourist activities. I shook my head and told them that being around them was a one-of-a-kind experience that I didn't want to pass up. At that, they smiled, staring into the windows of my soul with appreciation. I could tell they were as happy to have me around as I was to be around them.

"Since you like me so much," one of Rudy's friends said, "how about you help me do my job? I pass out fliers for a travel agency. I will give you half the profit. There is a scratch-and-peek raffle on each card and if a tourist wins, they get a free vacation in Bali. The only requirement is that they must be between twenty-five and fifty-five years old."

I laughed, jumped off the curb, and happily agreed to help. We flagged tourists down left and right for hours, but to no avail. It surprised me how uninterested visitors were in the locals. Granted, we were trying to get them into a time-share raffle, but it was all free and they could win an all-inclusive weekend if they simply scratched correctly. We walked the streets the rest of the baking hot day. It must have been ninety-five degrees with an absurd level of humidity.

"Man, it must be demanding to work day in and day out here to provide for your family," I remarked, wiping the sweat from my brow.

"You know, Jake, it is just life. We live in a beautiful place. I have lovely friends. Money is not important, you know? We just need it to eat," he paused and stared at me with a smile. Then we looked around at the tourists hurrying on with their days. "It isn't actually real, just digits in a computer," he continued. "Your people don't understand this. Money is fantasy; sometimes we believe fiction because everyone else does." He grinned wider. "Just because people say something is real, doesn't mean it is real. Love and friendship are of greater substance. You won't find lasting peace of mind in cash, if you don't have love. However, we impoverished Balinese have all the honey—love—in the world. Good food, smiles, and friends. Right now, I only have 42,000 rupiahs and this is for my whole family," he paused and pulled out his meager bankroll. It translated to six U.S. dollars.

I gulped. I had been worrying about living with four dollars, while he supported his whole family with six!

"I have a wife and three children. It doesn't matter if I don't have the money; one of my friends will loan it to me. One doesn't become poor from giving; they become fulfilled. We are all family here in Bali. We float in the same boat of poverty together. Therefore, we lend hands to each other. That is what life is about, isn't it—giving to others without expecting return?"

I couldn't have agreed with him more. I didn't have a response, except for a smile.

We continued hunting middle-aged couples for the time-share but without success.

"How often do fish bite on what you're offering?" I asked.

"Very, very rarely, and by rare, I mean as infrequent as tourists smile at me." He laughed, unconcerned by the lack of business. "Last time was this past month. But every time I do, I get fifty dollars and that kind of money travels far. You know, it is life. It is funny. We must laugh or become swallowed whole by the beast."

He spoke to me for the remainder of the afternoon and evening, introducing me to every one of his friends we passed. Later, we ventured back to the curb where Rudy and company gathered. Motorcycles raced past us. I wasn't aware of the time, although I did know it was late, so Rudy tossed me a motorcycle helmet and took me to my hotel. I thanked him. He told me he would call me in the morning on the phone he bought me earlier that day.

That he did, at 6:00 am every morning, and so I spent the next few days better understanding my new family.

That Monday I was able to get a wire transfer in Indonesian rupiahs from Western Union. Once I received cash, I offered it to Rudy and his friends. They refused and told me they didn't want my money, only my love and presence. All they wanted to do was direct me to a peaceful city in the rainforest called Ubud. And so I snatched my luggage and said my good-byes, promising to return on my way out of the country.

I was truly blessed to have made these new friends. Getting by with barely any money in a country I knew nothing about was physical proof to me that when we take chances, we are always rewarded more so than if we had remained safely hidden in our comfort zone. With the possibility that life could end at any moment, I did not wish to have any regrets about not having had the courage to discover, dream, and risk. I'd be getting in all my kicks before it's too late. Just before my heart stops, I won't wonder if I tried everything I could. I will know for certain that I lived life for love and adventure, never in fear and complacency. For those are the only choices.

That is what life is about, isn't it—
giving to others without expecting return?

Receiving Abundance

Ubud, March 17, 2011

I am realistic. I expect miracles.
—Wayne Dyer

I learned right off the bat that it's not safe to kick monkeys. While walking through an animal preserve, I saw a child stomp on one, only to be bitten and wrestled to the feces-infested ground before being rescued by his mother. And while I watched those monkeys, it reminded me of watching political debates on TV.

On that note, I left for a local restaurant. There I sat on the stone floor. The brown bamboo tables were only a good foot off the ground. I inspected the native paintings on the walls while I rested my hands on the bamboo table. I placed my order for noodles and vegetables. I drank my tea and observed my surroundings. The restaurant was constructed of bamboo with a concrete foundation that met the gray stone street. A local man with gray hair to his waist walked up the nearby stairs

"Hello, my friend, I am Dewi," he said.

I returned the warm greeting, then asked, "Are you from Bali?"

He shook his head. "I am from everywhere. Born here, in Indonesia, but I am connected to the entire world."

I nodded to show that I understood, as he continued, "Every piece contains the whole. All of us are interlinked."

Dewi's smile spoke of gentleness and wisdom; the rest of him advertised a wonderfully carefree attitude. As it turned out, he had spent ten years in San Diego, my hometown, teaching Balinese musical culture at a private middle school. He spoke exceptional English. One way or another, we got to talking about meditation. He proceeded to tell me that he was a healer in the village and performed practices for the sick and injured. I was excited, but not surprised. I expected to meet interesting people, and so it happened time and time again. Along my travels I had been touched by synchronicity so often that I knew to expect it. "Coincidences" became messages from the unseen—like angels without wings, satisfying intermissions of life from a deeper level. They were omens.

Dewi invited me to his home after my meal to meditate. I accepted the invitation. I could see his shining soul echo through his sunny eyes. They had something hiding inside, something powerful and magical, and I wanted to know him better.

Once we parked his motorcycle, I looked around. The homes were bigger than Rudy's in Kuta, perhaps twice the size. Still, all were made out of gray concrete and stone, except wooden doors. The streets were narrow, barely wide enough to fit a typical American SUV. We entered his home, and I instantly felt at ease. It smelled of incense. The walls were covered in beautiful paintings of gods and goddesses. I was quick to learn that he was not only a musician and healer, but a painter too. He struck a match and lit a few more sticks of incense.

"How do you feel?" he asked.

"Comfortable. Relaxed. At home," I replied. "How do you feel?"

"Like nothing." He paused for a long time, and closed his eyes for many moments. I did the same.

"I feel like the smoke rising and drifting wherever the wind blows," he said in a low tone.

Dewi was a skinny man and walked with a slight limp. He spoke softly. His words were easy like a flute. I felt ecstatic at the universe's offerings in response to my desires to further my understanding of life. Power surged through my body, and I felt I could accomplish everything.

Dewi spoke, "We are here to make others' lives better or else our life is meaningless."

From the corner of my eye, I watched the smoke rising. I nodded, indicating that I wished for Dewi to continue speaking.

"Without courage one can never realize their destiny.... What is everyone waiting for?!" he asked with wonder.

I laughed from my comfortable seat on the bamboo rug. Then it was silent. I looked around at the concrete walls and watched the incense float.

"How do we change the imbalances of the world?" I asked. "Or will that come naturally when we all begin to follow passions and realize our capacities?"

Silence.

I watched the smoke rise from the incense. He smiled and then closed his eyes. "Let the greedy do as they please," he stopped and smiled wide. "We all have it coming back to us. We must take responsibility for our own actions and thoughts, Jake. The way to improve the Earth is to change you. Find your passion; we all must."

I nodded, telling him that I wished more people in America followed their hearts, because then we could change the world.

"You must write a book about traveling to help them," he said very seriously.

I smiled, but said nothing.

"You can do it," he said softly but with enthusiasm. "Life is simple. Now we are beginning to awaken to the greater aspects of ourselves. The dreamer is awakening. Join the awakening and help the human race!"

I was awakening. Throughout my travels, I had seen that when we ask from a pure place, we receive whatever we need. With my heart open and willing to receive, I invited abundance into my life and it came to me in various forms. And here it was again.

Dewi continued speaking: "When you wake in the morning, it is most important to ask yourself: *How can I be of service? What are my reasons for living? How can I maximize my potential? What are my intentions and dreams?*"

This is something I would do every day for the rest of my life.

I learned then that when we ask, we always receive. I expected my everyday needs to be met, expecting the answer to every problem, expecting abundance on every level...and so it happened time and time again.

First Sight, Old Friends

Gili Trawangan, One Poetic Week Later

> *Could a greater miracle take place than for us to look through each other's eyes for an instant?*
>
> —Henry David Thoreau

After spending the last week meditating with Dewi and writing poetry, I headed to a port town, Padang'bai. I had heard from tourists at a computer lab that you can take a boat to the beautiful island of Gili. Something was calling me there, but I didn't know what. I listened anyway.

I jumped off the boat onto the shore of Gili Trawangan, Indonesia. I was some two hours off the coast of Bali. The crystal-white sand reflected heaven's imagination. Nearby islands with serene green mountain backdrops put the cherry on top of what appeared to be the universal heart's painting of bliss (if it were to have a location in space and time). Smiles from locals spoke to me before their words made acquaintance with my ears.

I wasn't exactly sure whether I was dreaming or not, until I felt the weight of my bags on my shoulders. I mused to myself how all of the belongings I lugged from place to place really limited my freedom, but those thoughts quickly passed. This image of heaven made it somewhat difficult to process reality. The clapping of horse hooves on the stone road shook the daydream from my hair. No cars. No engines. No pollution. It was a land where thought actually played a part in the creation. It is illegal to have a motor on the island.

Hours, minutes, thoughts, and labels began blending together at an unworldly pace as I walked through the small island, which was only three kilometers in diameter. I searched for a place to put all this "stuff" that seemed to collect into bags from which I had previously sought identity.

Would others stare at me if I threw away all my belongings, stripped myself naked, and jumped into the ocean? I wondered.

Probably so. I reconsidered my options.

I purchased a room at Banana Homestay for seven dollars a night with breakfast, in a seemingly appropriate location less than one minute from the water. After quickly placing my bags down, I stepped back outside underneath the lone tree in the homestay's patio to talk with the locals who I connected with so deeply when I originally approached. Overcome by déjà vu, I felt like I'd known them for millennia. Ironically, enchanting music swept me off my feet moments later, which surprised me because I'd already felt like I was floating. I eagerly began to absorb the music in the nature of my surroundings.

"You've got a lot of life in your eyes," said an Indonesian man I would later come to know as Duel.

Tossing the potato of poetic introduction back at him, I said, "I equally see the light reflecting through the windows of your soul." I smiled.

I was not sure whether he smiled in response or if lightning shot out from his being, engulfing my vision. Either seemed plausible. Duel put his arm around my shoulder and guided me to toward the music and the seats full of locals, only a few feet away, near the bamboo fence. I pulled out my harmonica and followed along to the magical rhythm being produced by my long-lost brother, whose name I would later learn was Ari. Our souls danced before we exchanged words.

"You aren't like most other tourists, are you, Jake?" one of the locals I had joined asked me. I wasn't surprised by the question. I'd heard it plenty before.

"I come for experience, to learn your culture," I explained. "So if that is abnormal, then consider me an outcast."

Laughter clouded my ears, and I thought I heard one of them say that tourists go there to get drunk and sit in the sun.

Johnny, Ari's cousin, added through Ari's translation, "They ignore us like we are some kind of dangerous cartoon."

I hoped that I could rewrite their beliefs on what they thought of Westerners. And as far as I'm concerned, I did more than just that. I had rediscovered forgotten family. I recognized them, although we had never met. It was almost too bizarre to think that some people can live under the same roof for years and never really meet, while two others, at first sight, are old friends. I reminisced on such a truth while I rested in bed looking up at the stars in the sky that night. *Where the heck is the ceiling?* I wondered.

My days faded into moments. The moments became full of time spent with the locals just near the fence of my homestay. Bamboo benches and tables set the scene. A few feet past the two-foot fence and beyond the dirt ground rested the most authentic warung (food stand) I had encountered during my many months abroad.

Food in Indonesia at similar stands ranged from about one to two dollars per meal, but at this warung, food was half price. I was the only "tourist" who would eat there, and I did so sparingly since the sanitation wasn't all that great. It was a great place for the island residents to get cheap food. I had learned through conversation that the average local earned less than twenty American dollars per month. In the case of the teenagers around my age, it was more like twenty bucks every two or three months. Once the money was made, they would leave by boat to the island of Lombok, about an hour away, to give it to their families.

I learned that no one is born on Gili. They come for jobs created by tourism, sometimes as young as six years old. Most of them come from Lombok Island. However, Lombok is so impoverished that they have very little economic security. But some families will scrounge around to get enough money to send their children to the neighboring island of Gili for work. When they have enough cash to help the family, they can return by boat to Lombok. Their home becomes the island of Gili. This isn't an awful lifestyle if you are a wealthy tourist, but if you are an Indonesian sleeping outside without food in your belly or a shirt to protect you from the bugs and the rain, it can be rough.

I imagined what it would be like to be six years old and be sent by my family to some unfamiliar land to earn income....

The only item I have is the pants that cover my legs. The only way to make money is from the visitors to the land, but I don't speak their language. I sleep outside. I have no iPod to put me to sleep, so instead I cry my body to rest. Tears become lullabies. Hunger subsides with the itchiness of mosquito bites that smother my unprotected body. Rain falls on me. Since the trees have all been chopped down to make way for buildings to accommodate tourists, there is no wood for a fire. I roll on my bed of sand and rock, attempting to find comfort, but the mud from the rain clogs my vision. Morning comes, but there is no breakfast waiting.

Finally, I meet a friend who is willing to share. The two of us walk around the island day and night with a backpack full of woven bracelets we attempt to sell the next morning. Every now and then someone buys one. If they do, they try and cheat me out of the little money I am making by slashing the price in half. I must share the profit with my friend. I must also pay back another man for the backpack and bracelets. Not to mention a hundred other locals are selling the exact same items as I am in a one-mile radius. When I make a few rupiah, I can eat a bowl of rice for dinner.

The years flash past. I grow older. I am now twenty-three. I have learned English and have been able to survive on the streets. I now work in a homestay for tourists and sleep on the tile of the patio. I boat back and forth between islands as soon as my pocket fills with the weight of any paper money, so that I can give it to my family. *"No honey, no banana. No fruit, no fun."* My friends and I laugh about not having anything. Laughter acts as a drug to counterbalance all the miseries from poverty that a human inherently receives when they are a product of a world where a few indulge at others' expenses. I see everyone taking, but no one giving. I would give, but I have nothing of substance, except love. Therefore, I give twice as much love and three times the smiles. I think, *Why can't the currency of the world be based on love and positivity?* If it were I would most certainly be a millionaire. I block out my anger, occasionally puffing a few joints of ganja to forget it. I can feel dehydration and a lack of concentration from the heat. I peak into my pocket, but the wallet is empty. Equally empty is my family's bank account, though it is abundantly full of love. I try to pay for water with smiles, but in a world of greed, no one takes the offer.

One day a white tourist with long blond hair and a Bob Marley T-shirt approaches my homestay. Our eyes meet and I feel he is one of my kind. He puts a few bucks in my pocket by purchasing a room. He tells me that I live in paradise. I smile, thinking, *If only you knew all that we go through on a daily basis.*

He puts his bags full of all the clothes and belongings I never had into a room I've never been able to afford. He walks back and smiles, putting his arm around me. I sense he may be different. I feel he is already family, although I have known him for only a few minutes. I look into his blue eyes and tell him, "You've got a lot of life in your eyes."

He smiles back and introduces himself as Jake Ducey. He tells me that I am his friend and he has come to learn my lifestyle and culture. Music from my friends nearby takes both of us away beyond words. My new friend and I enter the transcendental realm of music as it speaks to my heart.

It was almost too bizarre to think that some people can live under the same roof for years and never really meet, while two others, at first sight, are old friends.

Almost Dead, Fully Saved, Completely Thankful

Lombok, March 29, 2011

What if today was the last day of your life?
—Kute Blackson

I awoke envious of the rainbow birds who sung good morning with unmatched freedom. For many days I would simply roll out of bed to spend time with my friends and brothers. With sweet acoustic melodies as a backdrop, we filled one another in on how it was to live life in our vastly different environments. My friend Ari, who spent most of the time on the guitar, had been educated in English far beyond anyone else and was very interested in my way of life.

He rifled questions at me faster than I had time to respond: "What are relationships like with girls in America? What's it like to have economic freedom? Why are you here when you live in California where it's so gorgeous?"

I was as awed by Ari's lifestyle as much as he was with mine. The days passed by with a half dozen or so other locals lounging around with us on the patio to my room. Ari often acted as a translator. "Why don't you ever do tourist stuff?" they wanted to know.

I laughed hysterically, telling them that I believed being a tourist should be about understanding new cultures and truly submersing ourselves in the lifestyle of our desired destination and not about going to fancy restaurants and bars.

Even though I had picked up some Indonesian quickly, verbal communication was often difficult. As had been true in other places, smiles and laughter spoke much louder than nouns, verbs, and adjectives anyway.

During our conversations, which Ari translated, I learned that each of the locals had as tough a life as the others. Some of my friends were providing for seven or eight family members. The stress on their lives was noticeable. It was giving me a whole new appreciation for having the money to quite literally get on a plane and fly where my heart longed to be. I was realizing that when we are born with certain privileges, even ones as simple as running water, we often become dull to the gifts they are.

Early one morning, one of my friends approached the patio. His name was Will. His hair had been dyed red from its usual brown and his eyes were bloodshot.

"Are you alright man? *Apa kabar?* What happened to your hair?" I questioned.

"You know 'ice'?" he responded with a tired smile in pretty good English.

I shook my head; I did not understand.

"It's meth…keeps me awake…I have no home to sleep."

I gulped awkwardly and asked, "How does that explain your red hair?"

"Much paint at the *warung*," he answered, referring to the local food stand. He ran his hand through his colored hair and smiled.

I looked at Will intently as he headed off into the day. I wished to tell him that it was an awful decision to do meth, but for some reason I couldn't. I just felt sorry for him, but I knew he was not a "criminal in spirit." Sitting there on the patio, I thought that in no way do I condone meth use, but at the same time I couldn't judge another on how they should live their lives. Besides, I had been given a serious reality check into the agonies of poverty. It made me cherish my life of privileges. It made me want to raise money to build a school on the island so that the locals could get better jobs and not resort to drugs. While I watched him suffering, I asked myself, *What right do I have as a human being to judge another on his choices?*

My nights of contemplation blended with days of education. I was receiving a firsthand degree in poverty, friendship, music, simplicity, love, and appreciation. Not only was I witnessing true poverty, but I was also experiencing the purest form of friendship. Companionship is something that can't be learned in school. Without understanding it, one really hasn't learned anything at all. So we were all giving to one another without expecting any form of return, other than to see a smile. I began to realize this wasn't out of the ordinary, but rather a way of life for Indonesians.

"Listen, Jake," Ari approached me one day while Duel was back in Lombok, after earning enough money to return to give it to his family. "My cousin Johnny and I would like to invite you back to our island and village in Lombok to meet our families and see where we live. We would enjoy so much to take you to our favorite waterfall and share with you the fruit from the trees in our backyard. We can go by boat and leave tomorrow."

I was elated by their invitation. I truly felt like part of their family. I was at home, although I was away from home. I accepted.

"We are honored to have you as a guest. You won't see any other white people the entire time we're on our journey. It will just be Indonesians," Ari said with a laugh, testing my reaction.

I told him I would be fine with that.

The chirping of the crickets announced the commencement of nightfall. It was decided that I would travel with Ari and his cousin Johnny to their village. I would meet their family, see their homes, and experience the beauties of their lifestyle.

The next day sprang up like all the days before it. This time I was on a boat watching the mountains flirt with the horizon. I felt like I was sitting on the frame of a breathtaking photograph. All the moments leading up to this moment had seemed surreal. *Why should reality set in now?* I wondered to myself.

We poured out of the tiny wooden boat onto the shore of Lombok. There was a little asphalt street filled with horse-carriage taxis and a few old vans. I looked around. Most people exuded warmth and hospitality, regardless of whether or not they spoke to me. I exchanged smiles with many and felt at ease.

Island pace was slow and I gladly joined in, making up for all the times I had sped through my surroundings as a kid. For the first time ever, I walked so slowly that I nearly forgot I was walking in between steps. I had even watched my new friends fill their bellies with laughter rather than food for the morning.

I proceeded to inspect the landscape: a few small, white, wooden buildings, loads of horses carrying cargos of food, a few white vans transporting people from the docks, and one long black asphalt road that led us from the shore into town. I looked beyond it all toward the huge green mountains in the background that poked approaching rain clouds.

I watched Ari flag down one of the white vans for a ride into their village. We sat in the bed of the truck on brown wooden planks. Aside from an occasional hole in the road that made for a few bumps, the ride was smooth. My thoughts dissipated while we hopped off the van in the village. Whoever saw me stopped what they were doing to study me. I smiled to assure them I had come in peace. Most smiled back; occasionally some didn't, probably because they were bewildered by my presence. We walked past a reggae bar and "the dudes" inside threw a hang-loose sign. I was welcomed.

"*Selamat sore!* Good Afternoon!" I hollered.

They smiled in appreciation that I was speaking their language. Next, we walked down a clay path between the divisions of concrete stacks that were family units. The path stretched out for a few straight miles, with homes on both sides. Many looked abandoned. Larger than the homes in Guatemala but smaller than Dewi's home in Ubud, these houses were very old gray structures with concrete walls and roofs. A few had metal gates intended to barricade their property, but they were mostly broken.

"Turn here. This is my home. This is my family," Johnny said eagerly.

Johnny spoke small drops of English, and although we couldn't always communicate fully, we seemed to understand each other through laughs, body language, and demeanor.

I took a deep breath in order to soak it all in. The instant I stepped onto their concrete patio, Johnny's mother smothered me with a hug. His sisters proceeded to engulf my being with love by hugging me once, twice, four times.

I introduced myself in Indonesian: "*Siya nama*, Jake."

"You speak Indonesian?" asked his sister who had studied English.

I told her only a little bit, but still she giggled with excitement.

We sat on the inflexible concrete patio. Johnny's mother approached with a mat for me to sit on because I was their honorary guest. I attempted to decline because it was the only sitting pad. Ari made it clear they would take offense. Their eyes were fixed on me. Then I excused myself to the bathroom to take a few breaths. Looking to open the door, I realized there was none. No water either. A concrete hole in the ground full of previous human waste awaited my bodily fluids. I could see bacteria and other fungi that didn't look the least bit healthy for my host family to be exposed to. I took another breath and sighed.

I reentered the circle of endless love. I smiled as wide as I could to express my gratitude, rather than demonstrating it through words. Just at that moment, Ari turned to me: "Johnny's mother would like to go with you on the motorcycle to the markets to purchase lunch."

I nodded and started laughing to myself because I knew that his mother and I wouldn't be able to communicate more than fifty words. I attempted to hop onto the back of the motorbike, but my laughter tipped me off the seat. I hadn't even dreamed of such an experience. Locals sitting on the street watched me like they would TV as I attempted to regain my balance. I hopped back on and waved to them. It seemed I was the village's entertainment for the day. We drove off as Johnny's mother, Leas, muttered Indonesian words that I didn't understand in the least bit. I responded with laughter.

I had never felt so out of place, yet so at home. I had heard many stories from various tourists I'd met about the dangers of entering areas without other Westerners. I never felt the least bit worried. Instinctively, I knew I was safe here with these people.

When we jumped off the motorcycle, I brought myself back to the present moment. We approached the market. It was a tiny wooden corner shop that had sleeping quarters in the backroom for the family. The locals there spoke no English at all. I could tell they were talking about me because I understood a few of the words. I smiled wider.

Johnny's mother and I sat down at a wooden picnic table to wait for the food we had come for. A teenager around my age approached with a high-five; he also had on a Bob Marley T-shirt. As he walked away I called, "*Terima kasih!* Thank you."

I watched the women chop up fresh rice links, purple taro root, and vegetables. They stacked each slice diagonally on top of the other in a way that caught my eye. Occasionally, Johnny's mother would say something to me in Indonesian. I'd just nod my head.

Once they finished bagging our food, which looked like enough to feed ten people, I paid for the lunch. It was about five dollars. In the areas without tourism, the cheap food prices are slashed in half. We headed home to eat. I ate two of the four bags. The girls laughed at me while I nearly developed an addiction to their purple delicacies.

With our bellies full, Johnny, Ari, his sister, and I decided to set off to the waterfall. Johnny started the motorcycles. Ari got on the back of Johnny's. I plopped myself on the back of Johnny's sister's motorcycle. We began. Soon after, I paid no more mind to the people; I had become lost in the mountain's green rainforest. Rice fields met the bottoms of the mountains. Clouds moved in slowly.

It was raining lightly, pattering on my face, which didn't bother me at all. It just put the exclamation point on the rice fields and pastures. As we wound our way up the spiral mountain, we passed through small villages planted on the beginning banks of the lush mountain. People sitting on the overhangs of their shops waved to us as we rode by. I enthusiastically returned the gesture from my perch on the back of the bike. The higher we climbed, the heavier the rain became. It splashed my face refreshingly. We parked at the top of the mountain, beneath the overhang of an abandoned bamboo shop. The rain picked up with bigger drops. Then we walked off the muddy path into a rock-climbing area that was without a designated trail.

My friends grabbed my shoes and backpack, so I would have more traction and focus, since the water was coming down steadily. The steeper we climbed, the easier it got because I gained more confidence. Except for an occasional slip on the wet moss that lined our uncivilized road, I was managing better than I thought I would. I knew that one bad fall could result in serious injury. The rocks tumbled into the river below. My friends were clearly experts at climbing and probably hadn't realized it wouldn't be second nature to me as well.

Ari joked, "Jake, it's okay, you are only human, and you ascend slowly. However, we are like monkeys, we can do this in our sleep."

Ari's levity eased my mind, which had been telling me that this hike was a bad idea. I could hear an exotic waterfall raging in the distance. As soon as I released my fear, I immediately realized that I was in an amazing wonderland. The rainforest was playing Mother Nature's crashing song with the waterfall. I stopped to listen as crystal-clear water journeyed down a road of magnificent rocks enveloped in green moss. This remote oasis was unsullied by human hands.

My comfort level in this uncertain place was increasing, and I started to pick up speed through the adventure. A last, we had arrived at our destination. I watched as my companions took off running into the pool of unspoiled white water that came from the tips of the massive waterfall down into where we stood. I followed. Rather than dampening my spirits, the rain enhanced the moment, echoing through the arena of rocks that now capped us in.

The suspension of time made the thought of reentering civilization inconceivable. We swam and played around in the water amidst the rain, enjoying the downpour. Minutes seemed to turn into hours, and then the sun began to set through the clouds above the mountains. While I watched the day shift to night, Ari reminded us that we had to make it back for the night boat.

We had to dismount from the saddle of the camel-shaped mountains. By this time, I was feeling maybe a little too confident with my climbing abilities and decided to carry my own belongings. The rain was pummeling us harder than ever now. I laughed and stuck out my tongue for a taste. One drop, two, one million raindrops. *Man, I sure hope this rain stops,* I thought to myself.

Just at that moment my left foot slipped on a patch of moss. The green algae, which had been my climbing companion, became an unforgiving foe. Perhaps it was because I had laughed and stuck my tongue out at Mother Nature. My body smacked into the rocks and I began to tumble toward the river. I rolled off the compact ledge of small boulders and onto a bed of rocks. My hand clutched the ledge but hastily slipped off the wet surface. I continued to drop, instinctively curling up my body and protecting my head.

Death looked me in the eye, but I wasn't scared. My many months of adventures flashed in front of me, and I didn't regret a single choice I had made. I was consciously creating my destiny to the best of my ability, and somehow this was part of it. I accepted that. I hung in the air for forever. A voice told me I would be all right. Another said that I had followed my heart to the brink of disaster. My body slammed with a thud onto the rocks below. I swallowed immeasurable amounts of water as I fell into the river. I was lying there, helpless, on the outskirts of civilization. *All alone.*

Johnny's sister's scream forced my eyes open. My right shin and elbows were bleeding. My back ached, and my thoughts raced. I was sure I hadn't broke anything and was thankful that I had fallen from a great enough height to cover my head; my arms had absorbed the impact. I expressed gratitude to the universe for my safety; an upsurge of healing power flowed through my veins, temporarily relieving my aches and pains. I took several deep breaths, and I could see that I was about ten feet below Johnny. He stood above me with a face of desperation, probably playing scenarios through his mind as to how he would save me. But there was no way to get to me without jumping off the edge. I looked for Johnny's sister, but could not see her. I figured she had stepped away from the rocks so as not to slip.

"Jake, are you okay?! Are you alright?!" Ari yelled with panic in his voice, running some fifty yards down the path I had just vacated. With that, I watched him jump off the rocks into a pool a far distance past me. His heroism brought tears to my eyes as I struggled to pull myself together. He landed in a small pond and ran toward me, but a barricade of rocks blocked him from getting any closer than about thirty feet.

I knew that the image of Ari jumping after me would always remain with me. It was the most resilient act of sacrifice I'd ever witnessed. *He put his own life in danger to help me.* I could've been carrying his corpse out of this magnificent rainforest, just as easily as they could've been carrying out mine. I cried for a few seconds and then my tears turned to laughter: Ari was more than human, all of them were.

Once I had gathered my senses, I realized that this was a lesson from the universe in recognizing the power of serving others. I smiled and looked up at Johnny. He was too high to reach. My arms hurt too much to climb. I was over a foot taller and at least fifty pounds heavier than him. If I were to jump and grab onto his arm, I would've pulled him overboard. We couldn't afford the chance of anyone else falling. Johnny signaled for Ari to head down the river toward safety. I attempted to mount the rocks that had victimized me. I had no leverage, and the rain made them insurmountable. The roaring water pounded my head, making it impossible to see clearly.

We had no choice but for Johnny to attempt to pull me up. He lowered his arms. I could see the desperation in his face as he tried to reach without tumbling over. His eyes were squinted shut in concentration. He leaned his buttocks backward, away from the treacherous fall, in order to offset my weight. It didn't feel like a good idea for me to grab onto him; I feared I would pull him over. But the challenges of getting back up on my own with my elbow swelling were far too great. The rain seemed to pour down harder, just to obscure my vision. I could no longer see his hands. I smiled one more time, trying to stay positive. I leapt and he grasped my arm.

First, my left foot fluttered off the ground. Then my right. I had no weight on the bottom where I once stood. I dangled in the air. He yanked me with sheer determination and Herculean force. It was as if he was the heavier person, and I was the lighter one. I couldn't have imagined a cleaner saving.

My two feet kissed the flat rocks of refuge. I pinched myself to be sure I was actually on safe ground. I smiled and hugged him. I grabbed him by the shoulders, spilling blood onto him. I tried to tell him that it was the most courage anyone had ever shown on my behalf. I couldn't find words. For a moment I thought I forgot how to speak while my tongue fluttered inaudibly Instead, I gazed intently into his eyes and showed what I felt by the light in my pupils. Then, I remembered I could talk. I looked at Johnny's sister with a slight smile because she still looked terrified.

"You saved my life! Ari? Does Johnny understand what I am saying?" I shouted. "He saved my life!"

"Yes, Jake, he knows," Ari called out from fifteen feet beyond. He was devastated that they had taken me as their guest and I had had an accident.

"We must get you back to Johnny's house to clean you before the boat leaves," he said.

By then my leg was covered in blood. My shirt was so muddy that I decided to take it off, because it was doing no good. I proceeded to march like an ant. My elbows were swollen and blue. When I looked at my wounds, I told myself I was going to be all right and that I would heal swiftly, remembering the *no-cebo effect.* I focused on the gratitude I had for my friends and their brave show of friendship. Such appreciation alleviated my pain.

I was still a bit in shock, of course. When I was finally able to concentrate on my breath, my heartbeat relaxed.

I opened up my bag to see if I had damaged anything. It was sopping wet. My camera was broken and my bundles of Indonesian papers that I used to practice the language were ruined. But I knew I would be fine. I just needed to get out of there without falling again. I smiled at them with assurance that my health was acceptable. During the motorcycle ride home, I played a mental game to block out pain and worry by becoming aware of my breath and feeling the energy within. My lungs peaked at every breath.

I joked with my friends, trying to loosen them up. They were clearly devastated that their guest had experienced such a scare. First they saved my life, and then they were saddened that the incident had even transpired. Besides, I knew it had happened for a reason, perhaps even a few.

Whatever the reason was, I would never know for sure. I guess the dream of life is ultimately its own interpretation. Nonetheless, I was certain that it would forever place an imprint on my life. We sped back to Johnny's home so I could be treated by his mother. When we arrived, she smashed up a green, spikey melon fruit and proceeded to clean my cuts. I drank milk from a coconut while I watched.

"Your mother is not here, so I am your mother," she said.

I laughed with appreciation. The love in their eyes brought tears to mine. Johnny climbed a nearby coconut tree and slashed up another fresh one for me to drink. They continued to apologize for putting me in a dangerous situation, but I kept assuring them that it was okay. I was alive. It was all that mattered.

Once Johnny's mother finished tending to my wounds with the skill of a medical expert, the three of us set off back to the dock. We had fallen behind schedule because of the incident, but were right on the mark to make the boat. We hurried onto the last water taxi. A local woman laughed when she heard me telling another person on the boat what had happened. Our eyes met in pleasure.

"The ocean is so clear here on Gili Island, just swim and it will heal well. Keep smiling, and you won't think about pain, fear, or worry," she said.

I smiled and thanked her for her advice, knowing it to be true.

Ari turned to me with his cell phone in hand. "It's broken. I forgot I had it in my pocket when I jumped into the river after you. I'm one of the few locals who own one. It was my graduation present for finishing my schooling in English. Although it's unfortunate, I would break a thousand to ensure your safety."

I could see devastation on his face. I put my arm around him and promised I would get him a new one. These were people unlike anybody I had met. The goodness they possessed was so beyond anything in the known universe.

"We believe that true friends must be willing to die for one another, or else it isn't a real relationship at all. If you aren't willing to lose your life to help another, you'll never really live at all," he said.

I smiled with admiration. I didn't have a response so I patted his shoulder. The boat touched the shoreline. We scurried off into the purple starlit sky to the homestay. Once we were back, I headed straight to my room to rest and take in the whole day. Within a few moments, a kind tapping on my door interrupted me. It was Johnny.

"Jake, I could tell by the way you were walking that you're hurt more than you say. You have a sore back and leg. Please, let me give you a massage. I can do them well, as I give them to tourists," he offered in half Indonesian, half English.

I laughed and agreed. He handed me a cup of local rice wine. I drank it to soothe my aches. I felt like a resident while seven or eight of them sat around smoking pipes and keeping my spirit high. But when my head hit the pillow, my mind traveled up the stairs of relaxation and peace to a summit normally not obtainable. Discomfort leaked out of my body and was replaced by relief and occasional sadness that I would soon have to leave my friends to head back to Bali for my bank cards. When he finished, I was exhausted and went straight to sleep.

Besides a few sore spots, I awoke the next day feeling grateful for my life and the friendships I had made. I stepped outside into the bright sun and climbed into a hammock. I began the morning by calling my mother. I longed to see my family.

"Jake, is everything all right?" she sounded worried. "Around eight last night, I got an eerie feeling that you were in danger. I cried." She paused to catch her breath. "I called your brother to see if he had spoken to you…Are you okay?"

I thought about a book I'd read on ESP before I left for my travels. The term was originally coined by Dr. Richard Burton. It involves the reception of information that isn't gained through the recognized five senses but rather from deeper within the mind. It can also be referred to as the sixth sense, intuition, physic premonition, gut feeling, and so on. I found it quite interesting how many documented cases of "impossible" extrasensory perception there were. And my mother's intuition was a prime example that we *really* are all connected on some energetic level that we cannot yet comprehend. Everything I had learned in Guatemala and from Dewi in Ubud was on the mark. I smiled.

With a laugh, I assured her that I was okay but that I did have a serious scare. I tried to convey how touched I was by my friends' display of bravery, but words could only make a divine mockery of it all. It was one of those times where human explanations are immediately tossed out the window. All that was left was a feeling, a sensation that had yet to be defined. It was some mixed vibration of disbelief and love that ran through my veins. I had thought I'd already gained a new appreciation of life, family, and opportunities, but it had been taken to an all-new extreme.

I could tell my mother was very worried, but I also knew she was beginning to understand that my travels were for a greater purpose that we would both soon understand. She urged me to relax with the locals, to not go on any hikes, but to stay calm. I told her I loved her and that I would. We hung up.

After the phone call, I went directly to Ari and Johnny, who were at the food stand next door. I needed to thank them again. While I walked, white clouds rolled in like marching soldiers covering up the sun. When I approached I hugged Johnny and Ari, who were playing guitar under a skinny tree. I looked them in the eyes. Tears slid down my face. I knew they understood. Just then, Johnny unstrapped from his neck a necklace made of black twine with a small portrait of Bob Marley hanging from it that he bought the day before with the money he had been saving for many months. He caressed it, and then passed it to me. "This is for you, my brother," he said.

I expressed many thanks and immediately put the necklace on. He smiled.

I knew they understood how much their friendship meant to me.

"You are unlike any tourist we have ever encountered," said Johnny through Ari's translation while he took a step back to admire his necklace on me. "You have made a genuine attempt to get to know us and our way of life. Our purpose is to live for others. When we do, we fulfill ourselves along the way. You have left us content. And you, you are family."

I didn't have much of an answer besides to tell them that I was glad that I had the opportunity to come stay with them.

After we spoke for a few more moments, they went back to playing their guitars. The sound rang far and wide, attracting the ears of many of the other Indonesians I had befriended. We all sat in a circle and listened. Many of them smoked a pipe. Together, we welcomed the universal language of music. The acoustic melody washed away my sense of time. This would be my last night here. The following morning I had to pick up my bank cards at the Padang'bai post office. I didn't want to leave. I had found a second family.

The good-byes to my friends were tough. Six or seven of them gathered around my room; I gave them all my shirts and bathing suits, except for one or two. Johnny put his arm around my shoulder. "You are a true friend, Jake," he said.

I smiled and admired the heartwarming sight of my friends holding the clothes I had given them the way I used to hold my Christmas presents from Santa when I was a little kid.

When Ari and I were alone, I gave him fifty dollars (half of the hundred dollars I had remaining from a wire transfer) and told him to use it to replace his cell phone and to buy whatever else he needed. It felt good to give back, and I wished I could give more.

Ari looked at me, hugged me, and began to cry. I patted his back and smiled.

The following morning he insisted on carrying my backpack to the boat to spend more time with me. Although still bruised, I didn't really need the help, but his company was welcome. I would miss him and the others I'd grown so close to. At the boat, I hugged my friend good-bye, promising I'd return when I could. I felt saddened to leave but knew with every part of my heart that'd I'd return someday to help them.

Back in Bali, I tucked my bank cards away after receiving them at the post office and headed toward a local computer lab to check my e-mail. Joelle, the free-spirited girl I'd met at the campgrounds in Australia, had e-mailed me about meeting up in Surat Thani, Thailand, later that week for a meditation retreat. It felt intuitively right. My one-month visa was up at the end of the week, and so I decided to book a flight to Thailand for my next destination.

The next day I took a crowded bus to the airport. I was numb to any emotion that was not a byproduct of gratitude. My life had been saved and I had been given a new perspective about what it means to be "privileged."

If you aren't willing to lose your life to help another, you'll never really live at all.

Part Five

Thailand: Furthest Reaches of the Human Spirit

Already Happened, Already Done

Surat Thani, April 1, 2011

> *The secret is to shift our perspective of life by feeling that the miracle has already happened and our prayers have been answered...prayers of gratitude for what already exists, rather than asking for our prayers to be answered.*
>
> —Gregg Braden

I trudged through ankle-deep water on the flooded main street of the Surat Thani airport. My thumbs were up to passing cars in the drenching rain while hiding my backpack from the rain under a nearby overhang. I was attempting to get into town. All buses were shut down as were the entering and departing flights for the remainder of the day. But I had reunited with Joelle at the airport hours before, making the day a lot less chaotic than it seemed to be. Traveling with a like-mind made everything easier. I was thankful. However, millions of liters of water stood between the us and the monastery, which was some forty miles away.

After having experienced so much these past several months, I desired to get to the meditation retreat and just close my eyes. All I wanted to do was feel gratitude for how life would be when I returned to America. In my heart and soul, this book was complete, although I hadn't even begun writing it. I thought back to what I had learned about Tibetan monks who were able to heal cancerous tumors by chanting a mantra: "Already happened, already done." According to the monks, *anything is possible; we must only imagine that it has already happened.*

Although I had learned that I could manifest anything for the highest good of all through visualization, I hadn't yet discovered how to turn flooded cities into sparkling castles. This being so, Joelle and I had arrived just in time for the most catastrophic flooding in Thailand's recorded history. After quite some time, a sedan with tinted windows pulled over. The driver was a local woman around forty who spoke very little English. Still, she invited us in her car for free, dropping us off at the only hotel in the area with both a vacancy and an affordable price. We thanked her kindly.

The villages were saturated with rain. Only the main road we were on was not flooded. Farmers canoed through their property with only hope. The once-fertile land became a minisea.

The woman who greeted us at the hotel told us that we wouldn't be able to head back out of the city for some time. All flights had been sold out or cancelled for the night. We seemed to be stuck in the flood for now. It occurred to me that the earth was seeking retaliation for our poor treatment of the environment over the last few decades. We were experiencing more and more bizarre weather patterns than ever before. It was summer, and it should have been over a hundred degrees. Instead, it was cold and pouring rain. And if there was one truth I learned from briefly studying climatology, it was that increased carbon in the atmosphere meant warmer air, which meant that it held more precipitation and thus, heavier storms.

That night in the flood city of Surat Thani, Thailand, Joelle and I bought a twin bedroom to share for twelve dollars. Our relationship was strictly platonic; we were both traveling for something more than romance and sex.

While I listened to the rain in bed, I could still hear Fernando speaking in my ear: *Changes have to be made in our lifestyles to make room for our future.*

The rain didn't stop that night or the next day. We hid in our dry hotel room, and midway through the following morning we threw up the white flag, giving up the idea of trying to make it to the monastery. We decided to head out before the floods blocked the main road. Once we got onto the bus back to the airport and began the uncertain ride, we could see that the damage had grown substantially over the past forty-eight hours.

The bus was full of everyone in Surat Thani trying to leave. There must have been twenty-five passengers, and I could not see the driver's reaction to the floods. However, others on the bus were looking out the window in amazement and taking pictures. Cars were actually floating, and although I felt sorry for the ones it was affecting, I was not scared after seeing my whole life flash before me in Indonesia. I knew I would be fine, though I was very grateful to not have to deal with such a catastrophe. One lane of the main road was beginning to overflow, and for the last few miles to the airport, only one lane was still accessible.

I couldn't imagine having my land, home, and farm destroyed in a matter of days. I watched farmers swim through the ocean of muddy water to their crops to save whatever they could. Only roofs remained. My eyes were glued to the window. I held gratitude for all the blessings my family and I had experienced throughout my life, never having had to deal with a disaster of this magnitude.

On the way, Joelle told me that she wished to go to Chiang Mai, a city in the north. She had read much about it and had almost decided on originally going there, rather than where we were in the south. We decided we would head to Chiang Mai if we could get a flight. When we got off the bus, we shuffled through the ankle-deep water into the airport. Once inside, I took a few breaths and threw off my wet jacket for a dry one in my bag.

We approached the airline counter minutes later. "Okay sir, you are number twenty-three on the wait list for the flights this afternoon. I'm sorry to inform you all flights are full," the airline attendant tossed us unfavorable news.

"Don't worry, Jake. We will get on the next flight," Joelle said with assurance while we turned away from the desk. "I know it. Just imagine it, and we will get on," she said with reassuring enthusiasm while we rested against the side of a vacant wooden check-in counter a few feet away.

Anxiety-painted faces zoomed past us.

Although we were number twenty-three, we weren't worried. I removed my shoes and we walked barefoot to a pair of seats Joelle had spotted. The two of us had agreed to visualize ourselves getting aboard the next flight, so we sat still and closed our eyes, thereby directly affecting the future with our positive thoughts. I knew that those travelers who focused on their panic and exaggerated their predicament were only making life harder on themselves by reinforcing their concern. I wished to share the secret.

"Mr. Jake Ducey and Ms. Joelle McNeil!" a voice called out not ten minutes later. "Please see the airline ticket counter."

We jumped up with anticipation.

"Passengers who were booked for the next flight cannot get across the flooded roads," the attendant explained.

I took a deep breath, eagerly awaiting her next words.

She continued, her voice laced with disbelief. "I'm happy to say you somehow made it onto the flight that's boarding in forty minutes."

Joelle and I exchanged the brightest of smiles.

It was then that I felt closer to this strange human race. For the whole universe of heavenly hands was working on my behalf—so much so that it was undeniable. We couldn't contain our smiles as we made our way past the worried onlookers. We were on our way to Chiang Mai—a city in northern Thailand that I knew nothing about.

The mechanical bird rattled as we lifted off, sending Joelle into bottomless sleep. We would be landing sometime after midnight and had plans to find the nearest meditation center at dawn. I was glad to have a traveling companion, as I had been without one since Cole and Colton had headed back home three months earlier.

I looked forward to clearing my mind through meditation. I also hoped for clarity on how to organize the writing of my travel experiences. I contemplated this as the plane soared through the downy clouds decorating the orange sky.

When we landed, the moonlight illuminated the surroundings enough so that I could see the dry land through the window. I sighed in relief. *This* was where we were supposed to be. As we exited the plane, two enormous mystic mountains glowing like pyramids greeted us. They were the mountains of Chiang Mai.

We had the disadvantage of arriving during nightfall, as I had in many other places, and lost the privilege to seek a good hotel deal. We booked a room with twin beds at a hotel accommodation center from a man I didn't completely trust. My suspicions were confirmed when we arrived at our hotel and immediately knew we had paid excessively for it. The odor in the room was extremely unpleasant. I lit up a few incense sticks to mask the smell. The spiraling smoke, which rose like the DNA double helix, lulled us to sleep.

I awoke early. It felt good to have a night of rest, even if it was short. I was excited to begin the day because I knew we would find the exact meditation center we needed. Joelle was already in the shower, and I sat on my bed to meditate. I closed my eyes and focused on the rise and fall of my breath.

When Joelle got out of the shower, I learned she had already scouted out the most appropriate monastery: Northern Insight Meditation, a Buddhist monastery. I consciously expressed gratitude for the benefits of traveling with a wise mind. Joelle had found us a free program. No money was necessary at all. Part of me was excited, part of me was nervous, but I knew I *had* to do it. We agreed to stay for fourteen days of silent Vipassana meditation. From my understanding, Vipassana, which means to see things as they really are, was originally taught 2,500 years ago as a universal remedy for all imbalances. As I knew it, the practice was a road of self-transformation through self-observation by witnessing physical sensations and thoughts.

That afternoon I called my mother to tell her I would be out of touch for the next fourteen days. I also asked her to inform my brother and father, as I could not reach them. When I hung up, I thought about how she didn't understand my decision. My mom wondered why I would want to meditate for fourteen days when I was in a material world. I told her that if I wanted to make a difference in the world I needed a strong spiritual foundation, which could only come about if I understood the real workings of my own soul, body, and mind. She agreed to disagree. I told her I loved her and that I'd be out sooner than she'd know.

I had learned about Tibetan monks who were able to heal cancerous tumors by chanting a mantra: "Already happened, already done." According to the monks, anything is possible; we must only imagine that it has already happened. When we live more in our imagination, we give ourselves the freedom to wander into unfamiliar territory and we can create new possibilities and miracles. These imaginative meanderings become our future when we know it's possible.

Fourteen Days of Silence

Chiang Mai, April 2, 2011

Northern Insight Meditation Center (Buddhist Monastery)

> *One may conquer a thousand men in a thousand battles. But the person who conquers just one person, which is one's self, is the greatest conquer.*
>
> —Buddha

When my feet met the driveway of the monastery I knew there was no turning back. I was going to have to face all my doubts, fears, and judgments. I had embarked on a quest to the furthest reaches of the human spirit. Still, I was unsure whether I was entering a prison or heaven when we approached the front desk. All three hundred or so foreigners and locals were dressed in white. This would be no place for my Bob Marley T-shirts.

This is going to be too hard.... You have no reason to be here.... Just go home to America, a frightened voice shouted in my mind as I signed a strict agreement to not speak, leave, or write.

That was the voice I was trying to eliminate, my ego. But I was there to build my own path and not follow the paved road of our culture. It was then that I made a promise with the heavens to become whoever I was meant to be. I didn't care what was considered socially acceptable. I was going to be who I was. I just needed to officially meet myself, although I wasn't sure how that would happen. Yet I did know that "myself" wore the same clothes as me, so I knew before our first formal greeting that we had some things in common.

I sighed out my fear as I read, "*Fourteen days of silence, unless in communication with a monk.*" And with that, I scribbled my name across the contract. I said good-bye to my possessions that would remain at the office while I jiggled in the turbulence of worry from my ego. Just then, a bald Thai monk with a rather shiny head approached. He wore an orange robe and black sandals. He smiled once, but then his face became serious.

"Don't panic," he smiled again. "One mustn't cry before they hurt.... We humans lack the basic ability for extended solitude and silence. Mental development, or meditation, is a deeply personal experience. It doesn't matter if you are Buddhist, Christian, atheist, Jewish, or Muslim."

I showed no physical expression in response to his words, although I agreed with them. I looked around at the other five people who had checked in too, including Joelle. Aside from Joelle, who was Canadian, the other four were either European or Australian—three females and one male. A couple of them looked worried. There were separate dorms for the men and women at different ends of the property. This meant that I would not see Joelle all that much, which was disheartening, as we had developed a relationship where we could always make one another laugh.

The ancient-looking land was surrounded by a majestic four-foot red-stone wall that looked as if it had been there for thousands of years. The grounds of the center were gray cobblestone. Tall trees laced the walkways, and copper Buddha statues hung outside the meditation buildings near the front of the property. A large white temple sat in the middle of the grounds. The wooden doors were intricately carved, and small gold gates surrounded it. I could feel within me the sacredness of the temple and the surrounding land.

After briefly inspecting the area, we paced unhurriedly along the ancient cobblestone pathway toward the meditation courtyard, which was sectioned off by a wooden fence. A silver statue of the Buddha rested in the courtyard, symbolizing personal awakening. I took a few breaths and sat on the blue mat I had received at the office.

The unfamiliar birdsongs pleased my inner self, while my outer-self eyed the giant copper gong just outside the fence. That gong would send us to sleep at ten each night and awaken us at four each morning. I imagined hitting it so that I would be kicked out and wouldn't have to overcome the endeavor of fourteen days of meditation. I was scared.

"Silence, silence, silence," the disciplined monk who I was soon to name Mr. Monk said. He spoke in a quiet but firm voice. "Knowing, knowing, knowing! All please gather around as you begin various durations of stay here." He handed each of us a small black timer to track our meditations.

As Mr. Monk explained in nearly perfect English, our Vipassana practice was about being mindful of our feelings. It was to contemplate the happiness-suffering-neutrality of one's experience. That is, to acknowledge happiness and to know how happy one is, or to acknowledge misery and to know how miserable one is, or to acknowledge the neutral feeling that is neither happiness nor misery. As Mr. Monk explained, simply to acknowledge them brings freedom because our custom is to suppress and deny our feelings. And while in meditation, our minds may think of negativity. We then take that thought as the momentary focus of the meditation by acknowledging *thinking-thinking-thinking,* before returning focus on how the body feels, rather than the thoughts of the mind.

"We will begin in fifteen-minute increments. When the timer sounds, it will signal your switch between walking and sitting." He spoke like an enlightened drill sergeant, if they even existed. If they didn't, then Mr. Monk was the first.

We all stood straight with our feet flat and eyes open. The first fifteen-minute increment of a five-hour session began. I started the timer, which would become a sort of personal salvation. I stood back a moment, watching the others begin to pace slower than a snail on Valium. I wanted to run away. I wanted to go home. Instead, I walked slowly and patiently, one... foot...at...a...time. I occasionally lost focus and looked around at the incense and the trees in the distance. But I would quickly regain my composure and continue speaking to myself as we'd been instructed until we became comfortable: *Right foot lifting, moving, falling, putting down, left foot lifting, moving, falling, putting down, right foot...*Each step took at least five seconds before the foot reacquainted itself with the leaves on the ground.

"Exhale the confusion, judgments, and worries out of your being and inhale a new way of life. You cannot fully help and understand others if you cannot fully understand yourself." Mr. Monk paused and watched us with intense concentration, occasionally calling out people who lost focus. "It was Buddha who said that if all problems arise from mind, what is left when it is transformed?"

In an otherworldly way, Mr. Monk seemed to care for nothing except meditation and discipline to the practice.

I focused on the majestic cobblestones beneath my steps, trying to stay in full concentration of my practice. I noticed that each of us moved at different paces, some very quickly, some as slowly as me. I watched Joelle move at my speed. I lost focus and found myself looking at the Buddha statue instead of the ground, where I had been placing my feet. Nonetheless, I continued to move in virtually suspended motion.

One moment I'd be thankful for finally realizing the significance of traveling with purpose and intent, and then the duality of my mind would reactivate and tell me that this task was too difficult, that I needed to leave and go home before the two weeks were up. But my heart knew I'd soon be back in America fulfilling my dreams and that I had the power to complete anything. *Nothing* was too difficult.

I could feel the world changing, or was it me...or both?

The bleeping timer thrust its friendship onto me. It was a signal to switch to either sitting or standing. My legs ached like never before, but now they were resting upon the ground in sitting meditation, which I preferred. I listened to the voice, which guided me out of restlessness and into the psychedelic light show playing on the backs of my eyelids: "Meditation is a vacuum, cleaning the dirty and negative aspects of your mind. . . . Can you hear the crickets sing? It should be all your ears are focused on, not on all your thoughts and worries."

I followed the rise and fall of my stomach. I preferred sitting a thousand times over walking because I could dive deeper into the power within me. I focused on the light within. The colors of time and space are only physiological, but the light within is of another frequency entirely. It is a power that can guide us. We can capture *it*.

I imagined this light igniting my heart's magnetic field, which is much larger than the mind's magnetic field (incidentally, both fields can be measured by EEGs and ECGs). While I felt my heart opening, I realized that telling someone to live through their heart is not a cliché. It is actually possible! Then, my concentration shifted to the tingling in my left foot. I felt the liveliness of the energy pulsating through my body, which is all too often overlooked when the mind is racing with thoughts.

While hours in rotation between walking and sitting passed, a deep-seated feeling of fulfillment presented itself when I wasn't worrying about the discomfort. I knew the universe recognized me and was organizing a plan to help me realize my destiny.

During the last hour of meditation on the first night, in the exact same spot we had started, my mind said, "I don't think you can do it."

I battled doubts and physical discomfort to uncover dimensions of my mind I didn't know existed. The timer showed compassion when it beeped, but many times, I could've sworn it stretched the minutes into hours. Our ultimate goal was eight to twelve hours of meditation per day. When we finished that day, we had only completed five. Still my body was feeling the effects of stiffness and pain. My stomach growled with hunger. My ego wanted to leave.

The glistening blues and purples of the starlit sky sent me inspiration as I walked to my room. Crickets chirped with tranquility, and I smiled at the distant Chiang Mai Mountains.

That night, feeling drugged, I sat in the little white room on the sympathetic white bed sheets. I took off my big white clothes and hung them on the white hangers. I lay down on the quarter-inch-thick mattress and debated whether or not I was dreaming. Moments later, I lost touch with reality to an alluring vision of the future. In my imagination was where I would remain until the gong sounded.

You cannot fully help and understand others if you cannot fully understand yourself.

My Friend, Humor

Chiang Mai, April 3, 2011

> *That's what I call meditation. You simply stand aloof and just see the mind disappearing, like a cloud on a faraway horizon, leaving the sky clean and pure. And in that state arises your consciousness in its fully glory, in its full celebration.*
>
> —Osho

The morning gong echoed an unfriendly wake-up call. Not being able to set the snooze button, I rose like a hawk, spreading my wings to greet the day. It would be hours before the sun actually rose. Rather than fighting the situation, I embraced the fact that I was on my own for thirteen days, except to report at 4:00 pm each afternoon to speak to the abbot or teaching monk.

I pulled open the massive wooden doors on the monastery. Detailed carvings depicted stories of ancient tales that told the history of the monastery. I was the first inside. Frustration and fatigue faded in and out of my experience. Then I remembered what Fernando had said, "Consciousness is the intelligence of the soul. Clear the mind as to not have a diluted consciousness."

That morning I couldn't have been more pleased to hear the breakfast bell ring. My excitement subsided within moments when I saw the meal. Rice with water was slapped onto my tin plate. *Mmm, rice mixed in hot water,* I joked to myself, remembering that humor was the one friend that wouldn't betray me, even in the gloomiest of hours.

I sat at an empty table. Then a woman began scolding me in a language I didn't understand. She was short and talking words I didn't know and so I ignored her for a little. The words got louder...I realized that I wasn't supposed to sit where I was, as it was designated for the monks. My laughter couldn't have been the response the woman was looking for. I couldn't help it. There were too many rules to follow and being the disturbing element that I am, I was already breaking them. I journeyed away, by myself, or what I thought was myself—only to realize that when we think we are most alone, we are really surrounded by inner guidance.

I looked at the Buddhists living there permanently while we sat in the courtyard. People of all ages, including small children who began their monastic life at five, playfully laughed at me. It made me smile. I couldn't believe that kids as young as five were already in full practice of their Buddhist ways. They appeared to be of a breed of humans far from anything I had seen in my life. There were no faces of worry to be seen or people running to catch up to the day. I was in a different physical plane of existence, although I was in this world. It was an entire village built off the foundation that the primary objective was mental development and conscious awareness.

Then I saw Joelle and smiled. She did the same. I stopped examining my surroundings and chimed in on the rhythmic chant of thanks that occurred before every meal: "We must contemplate this food before eating, so that it is not gluttonously eaten, but for the continuation and nourishment of the body, for simplicity, peace, and freeing physical hunger and suffering. The wise who give out long health, happiness, brightness, and wisdom will receive it."

All my life I had been accustomed to tasting sweet, salty, and other flavors and sensations, so, my first bite of the soggy rice tasted like I hadn't eaten anything. I opened my mouth and felt my food with my tongue to be sure. I shoveled another spoonful to check that I hadn't imagined it all. Still, it had no resemblance to what I had been used to eating. It occurred to me then that unconsciously, for many years of my life, I had been receiving pleasure from my food rather than seeing it as fuel to keep the fire burning within. I hadn't always treated my bodily temple well because I didn't know any better. I became very excited to see how I could deepen my meditation practice simply by not only being cautious about my food intake, but by limiting the consumption of it as well.

As time continued, my natural high became more expansive. My dream molecules were firing, and I perceived the world as energy. I was walking straighter than ever. I was free. Then, without warning, I would think—about my family, about life, about leaving…and I would suffer. The thought that my family was the other half of me would bring me tears of pain. I'd been without them for too long. This particular day was my father's birthday, and I couldn't even call him.

Nonetheless, my natural high expanded, especially with a decrease in food. The experience of dreaming, which occurred day as well as night, brought me into a lucid sanctuary where all illusion fell away. In this state, I found myself wondering things like, *Is it day seven already, or still day two? Is life even real, or just a dream?*

I saw the truth of impermanence. One moment, I would feel lonely, fatigued, and depressed, and just an instant later, I would feel more alive than I ever had. I became conscious that I was creating my own suffering. My thoughts and perceptions were creating reality, and as long as I was reinforcing my uncomfortable feelings, then I was just that, uncomfortable. I let go of everything and rested in the limitless energy of my mind so that I could cultivate wisdom.

Consciousness is the intelligence of the soul.

Remembering the Truth

Chiang Mai, Day Three

> *Ordinary men hate solitude, but the master makes use of his aloneness, realizing he is one with the universe.*
>
> —Tao Te Ching

It was mid-afternoon on the third day when I observed the first shockwave from reality—the air was humid, the heat was hungry, and my mind was running. My legs were shaking. I was lonely and uneasy about having to focus on the moment without distraction. Then I entered the Abbot's room. It was serene, and the hundreds of flowers illustrated their splendor against the back wall. They absorbed the fatigue from my body.

I sat on a huge magenta rug near his dark-brown wooden desk. I spoke to Pra Ajahn Suphan and told him I'd had some peaceful sessions where I would stay completely in the present moment and therefore I wouldn't suffer. But then I would drift into thoughts about what I didn't have with me, and I would begin agonizing, even crying, that I was spending the majority of my time thinking about my family. I knew I was unconsciously creating my own suffering, but it was still difficult to stop doing it. I didn't yet realize I eliminated my suffering by simply watching all the thoughts, even this one now, and not doing anything but letting go and being aware.

Pra Ajahn Suphan's orange robe cloaked his body. He laughed when I spoke, as if he appreciated my remark. "Yes, impermanence is a way of life and law of the world. Circumstances come and go like the wind. You're deprived of all you love so that you learn to appreciate them more." He stopped to watch my facial expressions, which were calm and collected. "From meditation we no longer strive to build ourselves with our judgments about what's good or bad, but rather we remember that we are only seeking the truth of who we are. And so, when the mind doesn't have other distractions, we are able to observe it. This is the training of mindfulness, contemplating the body, feelings, mind and your intentions."

I nodded and while he paused to write something down, I looked around the room. There were heaps of fruit baskets I assumed town's people dropped off to him for his generosity of giving advice without seeking any pay. I watched a purple flower float in the gray stone water fountain just behind him.

"Your family is not here now; however, when you succeed, they will be proud and fulfilled that their son is experiencing life," he ended.

Like magic, inspiration washed over me while I watched light from his aura. I smiled and could smell the hundreds of flowers that covered the wall to my left. I studied the abbot's round glasses, which hung off his nose. In a matter of minutes he'd completely empowered me to get past discomfort. That is what self-realized people do; help others past their own life hurdles.

I wandered the gardens that night, appreciating the many exotic plants that bordered the cobblestone. The crickets chirping from their hiding places within the plant life relaxed me. I admired the golden elephant that adorned the gate. And I laughed at a patch of magenta-shaded flowers in the moonlight, radiating their dignity and commitment to love each moment.

I set my timer for one hour and I closed my eyes to meditate. Minutes passed. Colors splashed the inside of my eyelids, as energy flashed and morphed into newfound confidence. I wondered if God was finger painting in my field of vision.

"Bleep! Bleep!" the one-hour alarm on my timer rebuckled reality's seat belt just as I was dissolving into the universe.

I exhaled the density of space and time and instantly questioned whether or not to stay in the session longer, because I knew I could've floated further. But when I readjusted to my senses, I realized that the mosquitoes had other plans. I walked to the sparkling marble halls of the monastery.

I was eager to elevate the euphoria I had felt in the last session. When I closed my eyes, I could see spiral shapes of energy. My arms and legs fell asleep, but my mind stayed awake. My sensations turned to numbness. I was in the field beyond right- and wrongdoing. I was submersed in the potentiality that creates worlds.

Dear God, I said. *Thank you for being me!*

Rainbows and other unrecognizable images flashed within. I thought I saw a butterfly, and once I labeled it, the image faded. My mind reminded me, *Once you label me, you invalidate me.*

I could feel a hurricane of inner energy, "chi" or "prana," brewing. It manifested for me as particles of dust, and then an outline of a rainbow serpent shot forth. My body exploded in a zing of intelligent vibrations—which I later realized was *kundalini* rising, or *corporeal energy*, which had been unconscious but was reawakened. I was outside of space and time in a completely harmonious dimension. When I would give thought to what was happening, I would drift toward reality, but when I would just breathe, I would travel further away, feeling lighter.

A higher level of me was speaking: *When you are living in fear, worry, or doubt, you are cutting yourself off from the wholeness of your being. You are unknowingly living in fragmentation, because you're only being a fraction of who you are by not acknowledging the fullness of your capabilities. There are ultimately only two types of perception, love or fear. Love is the ultimate growth and developmental perception, while fear is the exact opposite. Follow your dreams with love, and the world expands to make them possible.*

I felt like my body was actually more of a radio broadcasting tower, transmitting frequencies into the world based on my thoughts. In return, I was receiving physical experiences and emotions. I saw that thoughts made physical things and real feelings. It was then that I truly knew who I was and what I wanted. I saw that life isn't complex. It's simple. We are all greatness, come from that greatness, and deserve nothing less than greatness.

In that moment I knew that all we have to do is just realize who we are, what we are after, and how we will begin. And then there is a certain redemptive force that making a choice has. Life responds to our intentions. It left me scratching my head when I completely realized that I had been told otherwise my whole life, and that we still are daily.

Why? I wondered. Then I took a careful look, asking myself: *When a child is born what is it that immediately takes it from its mother?*

The system.

I knew it was the same broken one that has led us to believe that greatness is something outside of ourselves.

Vocal chatter brought my senses back into the reality my body was in. I accepted the situation and refocused my mind on my breath. A few more blotches of incomprehensible sound flowed into my ears. A finger tapped my left shoulder. I turned meditatively and opened my eyes to the room. It was like I was looking through a kaleidoscope. Flashes of energetic color zoomed across my visual screen and reality wasn't definite. My body felt nimbler than usual. A monk stood in front of me, but his body just looked like a high frequency of light.

"Excuse me, my friend, but I have been trying to get your attention for minutes. It's past ten o'clock. It's time for me to close the doors for the night," he said softly.

I laughed blissfully and peered at the clock, only to see I'd transcended the physical realm for two hours. I had overcome all fatigue, discomfort, and loneliness. It was then that I knew from my own experience that the mind is, without a doubt, capable of achieving anything. That was the night that the universe personally told me that we could all live our destinies that were for the highest good of all.

There are ultimately only two types of perception, love or fear. Love is the ultimate growth and developmental perception, while fear is the exact opposite. Follow your dreams with love and the world expands to make them possible.

I'm Not There

Chiang Mai, Day Four

All matter originates and exists only by virtue of a force which brings the particle of an atom to vibration... We must assume behind this force, the existence of a conscious and intelligent Mind. This Mind is the matrix of all matter.

—Max Planck

The next day I woke up before four in the morning and was at the monastery to meditate before the gong sounded. I was inspired. More importantly, I was evolving.

I felt fifty feet tall, without worries, fear, or doubt. I asked the world to teach me, and it had. I sailed emphatically through the day with anticipation of speaking to Pra Ajahn Suphan in the afternoon. When I got there I told him about my out-of-body experience and all that I had learned.

He laughed wisely. I watched his eyes look through his head for the right words. "You see, impermanence really is a truth of life. One moment you are depressed, the next you are in bliss. However, there really is no such thing as *you*, for the idea of self is a concept that comes from an attachment to feelings, thoughts, emotions, objects, accomplishments, senses, and experiences, rather than just observing from a state of conscious awareness in the moment."

He pulled his glasses off and looked through the lenses like they were a crystal ball with all the answers. "The whole reason someone comes to our center is to understand and experience that firsthand. No one saves us but ourselves. No one can and no one may. We ourselves must walk the path." He paused to write something with his savvy left hand.

"A radical inner transformation and rise to a new level of consciousness is the only real hope we have in the current global crisis brought on by the dominance of the Western mechanical and competitive paradigm," he said.

Feeling inspired and uplifted, I studied the smile lines on his face, as he rubbed his hands together like they were kinetically sparking wisdom. He lived by the premise of an enlightened man—*that if you aren't making someone else's life better, then you're wasting your time.*

Gently, he thanked me before I left, and I saw the microexpression of pleasure he'd received from our talk, as if he wanted me to ask more questions.

I experienced the impermanence of the human experiment through the next few days, lifting in and out of alignment with the stream of life—sometimes succumbing into the rocks of boredom and discomfort. But then, all the sudden, it was different. I was aware of where my thoughts were leading me. I could redirect them before they shifted my mind too far away from my intentions. I was educating myself every day, or I was being aware and consciously dreaming.

There really is no such thing as you, for the idea of self is a concept that comes from an attachment to feelings, thoughts, emotions, objects, accomplishments, senses, and experiences, rather than just observing from a state of conscious awareness in the moment.

How?

How did we get here? How do thoughts appear?
Truth is so unclear.
Some say all structures are unstable.
Deceit is truth in a world of fables.
That all our beliefs are relative,
So we just can't be told how to live.
Could it be our attachments to images that's misleading?
Are we really awake, or simply dreaming?
Some say misfits and free thinkers are blinkers of knowledge.
That it's all a collage of illusion's mirage.
How did we get here? How do thoughts appear?
Truth is so unclear.
Some look at our world like a game of random coincidences.
Others see creation and manifestations brilliances.
Much is said but when I open my eyes there's no direction.
Can't we clear reality's mirror to see our reflection?
How did we get here? How do thoughts appear?
Truth is so unclear.

—Jake Ducey

Mucky Pants

Chiang Mai, April 12, 2011

> *There is no particle at the source; particles do not create other particles. The field of invisible intelligence is the soul-governing agency of the particle…As far as the laws of mathematics refer to reality, they are not certain, and as far as they are certain, they do not refer to reality.*
>
> —Albert Einstein

Each day the field of life around me was abundant in opportunity. When I would remember that, I would break free. I knew from the source of what I was that I appreciated who I was. My one-time mental prison had become a palace, where I could achieve what I needed. I could remember in economics class, when I wondered how I would break the bars on my mind's jail. I had done just that. I embraced the endeavor of returning to America and testing what I'd discovered. I was experimenting with all that hides within. And I wasn't scared, because I knew the truth: a master is someone who, in the midst of a parade of people, is able to keep their independence and speak their own heart. Those who do, realize their life purpose.

A few mornings before I was scheduled to depart the monastery, I stared at myself in the mirror for hours on end. The last time I had done it was before I left to travel, when I had no idea who I was or what I wanted. This time my reflection was different.

I was looking past my eyes, beyond the shapes. For the first time in my life, I could see who I was. I was peering beyond boundaries into the hereafter. Once I walked away from that mirror, the cosmic dream was discernible: *we can do anything if we imagine, if we believe, and if we act upon our intentions.*

Poetry and purpose flowed through my mind like a river. All my travels, tickets to fly on metal birds, and many miles across the globe were spent persistently uncovering who I was, and I had a sensation of accomplishment that weakened my knees. Yet it was quite interesting to discover that I had come to truly understand myself the most while in meditation, not while looking around in the physical world.

Nonetheless, I was some eighty hours from the culmination of the starkest endeavor I'd come across. I was thrilled while bathing in the sunrays. I watched a blue bird of happiness rest on a tree branch some three feet above me. I took it as an omen from the universe of more good things to come. There were a few clouds, and while the precipitation within them cooled and condensed, I did the opposite. I was expanding my unlimited potential into the material world. Meanwhile, the monks chanted their afternoon mantra. It carried me into the silent space between thoughts.

On the last night, while meditating on my mattress in my room, my soul spoke again: *You all didn't come here to earth merely to get life done with a means to an end.*

Clung! Clung! Clung!

The dawn bells woke me. Moonlight seeped through the cracks in the door. I opened my eyes with an electric smile, looking around at my ten-foot-by-ten-foot room of white walls. I wrapped myself in my white sheets and sat on the blue tile porch to awaken to the lingering stars. I watched a few other dorm room lights flicker on. The sporadic clouds passed speedily. It made it seem like the sky was moving.

I rubbed the sleep-buggers from my eyes and went back to my room for some yoga poses. This was my last day of silent meditation. I stood in warrior-two position with my legs wide, breathing deeply. I could feel stomach gas bubbling, and so I let it out my buttocks. Moments later my legs were warm and gunky. I convulsed into a fit of laughter then hurried off to the laundry room without suffering even a pang of embarrassment.

The rest of the day went quickly. My meeting with the abbot didn't feel long enough. I wanted to hear more of what he had to say and I had many questions. "Do you suffer when you're a monk?" I shot out the first question from my loaded barrel of curiosity.

He raised his brown eyebrows and assured me that all humans suffer, that we are all sentient beings, so we cannot eliminate emotions. We can become aware of our emotions, and then choose where to go from there with our heart. This is how we rise above being human.

I nodded and smiled to acknowledge appreciation for his answer.

"Does that mean we have the collective choice of how we want the world to be?" I asked.

He closed his eyes for a moment before adjusting his glasses. Then he shook in laughter. I felt like the rug below my knees was threaded in wisdom, as curiosity dribbled from my nose. "That's true. The state of the world is a reflection of us internally." He paused and pointed inward toward his heart. "To change the world we have to make changes in ourselves," he stated while smiling wide and chuckling softly.

He raised his slender arm as if to motion for my next question. I asked, "What are your beliefs about those who follow their heart? While reentering the Western world I get to deal with situations not as peaceful as here," I stopped and laughed, trying my best not to judge my Western world. "What's the best advice you can give someone who is creating their dreams and speaking their conscious mind?"

He scratched his head, laughing as well. He looked around the empty room with squinted eyes, as if he was showing me with facial expressions that it was a serious question. "My advice is to not speak your mind at all, but rather speak your heart." He lifted his finger and added his customarily soft chuckle. "That's the toughest thing for us as humans to accept, that everything is simpler than we think it to be."

He let out a burst of laughter, as if he had just given me his secret to life. I smiled at him and nodded, acknowledging that I understood the simplicity he spoke of. He took a sip of water from a clear glass, waving his hand gently to signal for another question.

"What is humanity's role in creation?" I wondered.

With a smirk, the abbot responded soft and slow, "To be caretakers." He paused, making sure I heard. "We are all individuated aspects of the Creator, Love, Life, Universe, Source, God, Buddha, Allah, Jesus, Ramakrishna, Force, Highest, and are here to experience this truth. *Darkness* only means that one has forgotten this truth and has subsequently developed fear and its many forms of greed, lack of compassion, anger, and jealously. Eliminate fear and amplify love." He stopped and raised his finger to signal an emphasis on his last sentence. "That will result in the shift to harmonize all life."

I smiled, putting my hands together in prayer position to acknowledge his time and wisdom. I told him I had no more questions.

Our session was nearing an end. He wrote a few things in his black notebook. Then he said in a firm, emotionless voice that I must reenter the world in the morning and not lose the flame that burns within. He said that the time is fast approaching when we will all shift our consciousness toward the truth: We are more powerful than we know.

Then he thanked me for coming to share my experiences with him. The moles on his shaved head looked like intelligent transmitters of information that whispered the words of the universe. His well-defined chin throbbed in discipline. I put my hands together once again to thank him. He did the same before

I slowly walked outside. I contemplated the air. Its breeze was soft and invigorating. A few stars had begun to show.

That night, a battery-charged waterfall kept me company in silence. I smiled. I had an aim in sight and knew that it was my time to enter the world with all that I'd found.

We are all individuated aspects of the Creator, Love, Life, Universe, Source, God, Buddha, Allah, Jesus, Ramakrishna, Force, Highest, and are here to experience this truth.

All Leaves Fall from Trees

Chiang Mai, April 16, 2011

I know where I'm going and I know the truth, and I don't have to be what you want me to be. I'm free to be what I want. And I know service to others is the rent you pay for your room here on Earth.

—Muhammad Ali

On the day of my departure, I stood for a moment on the path just outside the room I had been staying in. The tops of sacred trees had grown together, forming a pleasant tunnel.

I stood on the stones and thought about how I wouldn't miss staring at the blank white walls every day. My Bob Marley T-shirt made me feel colorful. Each hue vibrated at a different frequency of emotion, all pleasant but diverse energies. While I waved good-bye to the distant mountains, crackling afternoon thunder responded with nature's regards. Then Joelle walked past. When we originally signed the contract she had decided to do fifteen days. That meant she still had another day. I hugged her good-bye silently, trying not to break her time of silence.

When I walked away, my backpack nearly tipped me over. I had lost a lot of weight in the past two weeks, which reaffirmed my decision to return home. I had found what I was looking for. Life was at ease. My sails were set. The wind was at my back, and the world was in my lap.

I stood, transfixed by my surroundings. I would miss the cobblestone paths and ancient trees. When my eyes fell upon one of the monks in his orange robe, his eyes demanded my attention.

He spoke with a calm smile while the two of us took a seat on the steps of a storage room. "All of those bags must mean you are leaving. I can tell you are American. There aren't many of you here."

I laughed and told him that I had a destiny to pursue back home. I inspected his severely chapped lips and freshly shaved head, which was saturated with new razor burns, symbolizing his acceptance to the impermanence of life. Ironically, none of it seemed to bother him. I wondered if he even noticed. Then I asked how he knew I was American.

My question was met with a high-pitched laugh. "Americas always have the most belongings," he replied. "Oh, my brother, have no fear of leaving. The beauty of life is that we learn from experience, whether it's solitude or city life. Though everything we base the foundation of our reality on should be tested by our own consciousness. It's how we gain understanding."

I smiled with gratitude, listening intently. I knew that the two of us meeting was an example of the divine reason that he spoke of.

"All leaves fall from the tree. Whether they're old or young, it doesn't matter. When the wind comes, it blows many over. You look young...would you be satisfied with your life if you died tomorrow, here in Thailand?" he asked softly.

I was a little taken aback by his question. It wasn't my plan to die then without being able to put into practice all that I'd learned, but he didn't give me a chance to respond before he said, "We should all be asking ourselves whether or not we would have regrets if we were to crossover to the other side unexpectedly."

"I don't believe that's part of what I am meant to experience," I replied, maybe a little defensively.

"Oh, brother, it's a truth of life. It happens every day...in any city...to anyone." He paused to emphasize what he had said. "I used to be a travel guide for tourists, and four times, I saw

Westerners die on the spot from some health problems. That's why we must always do what we love."

I thought for a moment, and then told him I'd be home with my family and friends in five days. There I would carry out my life mission, not in Thailand.

"Yes, everyone has a different purpose. The tasks change for all. But we each have our talents. One person could be the best poet or the most patient mother; another could be the premier basket weaver, have the finest smile, be the purest yoga instructor, or the most inspiring teacher." He paused, without stopping his continuous smile once. "One could even be a paper stapler. It doesn't matter what it is as long as passion is present and we are following our mission and goal. That is how the near future will be—all will be operating out of pure happiness by loving what they do. We will have a world where all are bringing their innermost value into the material world."

I smiled, agreeing with everything he had said. I told him it was my passion to inspire everyone to follow their passion. But knowing that to listen is to learn, I quit talking and focused on the spirit in his eyes. He went on, "To be the change you want to see in the world, ask yourself these questions: *What are ten ways in which you are different from others? What is your unique purpose to benefit all of humanity? What is the primary motive behind what you want to do in life?*"

I tucked these question marks into my pocket for a later response and continued to listen as he spoke. "When we leave from each other's presence, we do not say good luck. *Luck* is a fantasy word that does not describe reality. There are no such things as coincidences.... We didn't meet by chance. You needed someone to talk to, and I sensed it."

I laughed wholeheartedly in agreement with his message and excitedly embraced this almost magical ending to my travels. The monk's words were ones I understood very clearly on all levels of my being, and I imagined that wondrous expressions were painted across my face for his delight.

He spoke softly once again, "In your life it took you until you traveled around the physical world for months before you found what you wanted, which was actually within yourself." He laughed. "Pretty funny! It's true, all begins *within* not *without*." He pointed at me playfully. "Now that you have found the treasures of your being, you must turn them into the work of the heart by sending your intentions out into the world and allowing yourself to receive the abundance that is returned to you."

His words were the exclamation point on all that I had learned.

"We will not thank each other for the time we both have given, because those who give will receive," he said humorously.

With that, the monk picked his petite body up, orange robe and all. He slowly moved his skinny and gentle body into a standing position. Then he gathered himself and leaned on the nearby tree trunk to the side of the ancient gong. He smiled one last time before walking away. I watched his back as he meandered out of sight, listening to his sandals rub against the sand on the cobblestone.

His wise words—like the words of many others throughout my long journey—added kindling to the fire within me. I would be a torchbearer for the West. I would spread the message to all of humanity of this universal truth: *We are powerful enough to realize any dream we have for the highest good of all; not only is it our responsibility to live our destiny, but if we do not use our talents to make a difference now, we will be the ones who witness the demise of our beautiful world.*

To be the change you want to see in the world, ask yourself these questions:

What are ten ways in which you are different from others?

What is your unique purpose to benefit all of humanity?

What is the primary motive behind what you want to do in life?"

Colton, Jake, and Cole with the children on last day in Guatemala

Cole, Colton, Jake, and Fernando (the shaman) in Guatemala

Fernando's niece, Evelyn, saying goodbye at the Guatemala bus

Jake's Mansion in Byron Bay, Australia

Tetsu (from Japan) and Jake in Australia

Rudy, Jake, and Rudy's cousin in Indonesia

Ari and his cousin and aunt in Indonesia

Johnny in Indonesia

Jake on last day in silent meditation

Afterword

Since 2011 I have stayed in contact with the shaman from Guatemala. Days before I met him, he had finished an outline for a school he wanted to build to educate, clothe, and feed the orphans of Lake Atitlan. It was no coincidence that I came to his town a few days after the completion of this outline. After that time my brother, Cole, and I have raised the funds to build his dream school, *Ixiim*, as well as build a home for orphans. Lastly, I have been taken aback by the invitation from *New York Times* bestselling author Greg Reid to be a coauthor on his book *The Rise,* which became an Amazon bestseller in September 2012.

To connect with me further, please visit www.jakeducey.com.

Many thanks and love,

Jake Ducey